Alexander A. Potebnja's
Psycholinguistic Theory of Literature:

A Metacritical Inquiry

John Fizer

Alexander A. Potebnja's Psycholinguistic Theory of Literature:

A Metacritical Inquiry

Distributed by Harvard University Press
for the
Harvard Ukrainian Research Institute

Publication of this volume was made possible by a generous donation from Anna Lewkut and Mykola L. Hromnycky

The Harvard Ukrainian Research Institute was established in 1973 as an integral part of Harvard University. It supports research associates and visiting scholars who are engaged in projects concerned with all aspects of Ukrainian studies. The Institute also works in close cooperation with the Committee on Ukrainian Studies, which supervises and coordinates the teaching of Ukrainian history, language, and literature at Harvard University.

Preface

Alexander A. Potebnja (1835–1891) was an outstanding Ukrainian intellectual of the nineteenth century. He not only greatly affected literary and linguistic scholarship in the Russian Empire and later in the Soviet Union, but, arguably, inaugurated formalist and structuralist theories in this century. My initial encounter with his theory, or what in the Soviet Union is generally known as *potebnjanstvo* (Potebnjanism), came in the 1950s, when I was a graduate student at Columbia University. At that time, convinced that psychology was the *Grundwissenschaft* for both the humanities and the social sciences, I found Potebnja's theory ostensibly psychologistic and thus validative of my conviction. Subsequently, as a result of my acquaintance with Husserl's phenomenology, I altered my view on the epistemological preeminence of psychology and reread Potebnja without psychologistic bias. To my amazement, I found him practically free of conceptual presumptions and, on the contrary, very much committed to the search for demonstrated proof. Historically, Potebnja's views on literary art are definitely inchoate; synchronically, unlike a great many past theories, they retain remarkable cogency.

Very little of impartiality has been written about Potebnja. The limited explication of his theory has been primarily due to the disinterest that modern literary theory, here emulating the exact sciences, has shown in its own past. René Wellek's sustained effort to present such a past is an exception rather than a widespread pursuit among literary scholars. In his compendious *A History of Modern Criticism* Wellek rightly perceived Potebnja's anticipation of Croce and Vossler as well as his pronounced influence on symbolist and formalist theories. However, given the limited space of his *History,* Wellek could not but limit Potebnja's theory to a reductive précis.

In the Ukraine, from the early 1920s to the present, Potebnja has been subjected to varied denigrations as well as hagiographic homages, reflecting vacillations in Soviet ideology. My study, then, is the first comprehensive analysis of Potebnja's literary theory in its inferentially amplified formulations rather than in its original terminological paucity.

From the organization of the material to its critical examination and evaluation, I have relied on the ideas, judgments, and methodological apparatus of current theories of literature, particularly those of the late Polish philosopher Roman Ingarden. My sense of the historical context of Potebnja's theory was acquired from Wellek's *History*. To these and the other scholars who directly or intertextually affected my views, I owe my deep gratitude. Should, however, my study contain factual inaccuracies or descriptive inaptness, my own inadvertence is to blame.

I am grateful to the editors of *Harvard Ukrainian Studies* for permission to republish the chapter "The Structure of the Poetic Work of Art," which originally appeared in the journal (*HUS* 6, no. 1 [March 1982]: 5–24). My manuscript was scrupulously edited by Irene Fizer and Diane Grobman, both formerly of Rutgers University Press, and Uliana Pasicznyk of the Harvard Ukrainian Research Institute. I owe particular thanks to Maxim Tarnawsky, also of HURI, for his professional attentiveness to the technical aspects of the manuscript and George Mihaychuk for seeing the manuscript through its final technical preparation. My secretary, Dagmar Jensen, typed the text patiently and diligently, a task which, considering my often illegible handwriting, must at times have been arduous.

New Brunswick, New Jersey
January 1986

Contents

Preface   v

Introduction   1

Chapter One: The Essential Being of the Work of Poetic Art   8

    Epistemological Constraints   8

    The Work of Poetic Art as Activity   11

    The Work of Poetic Art as Narration   14

    The Work of Poetic Art as Teleologically Charged Form   16

    The Word as an Analogue of the Work of Poetic Art   19

    The Conceptual Ambivalence of Potebnja's Ontology   23

    Conclusion   26

Chapter Two: The Structure of the Work of Poetic Art   29

    Structural Affinities between Language
      and the Work of Poetic Art   29

    Structural Constituents of the Work of Poetic Art   36

    The External Form   38

    The Internal Form   40

    The Content   44

    Conclusion   47

Chapter Three: The Modality of Poetic Forms   51

    Immanent Forms   51

    Intentional Forms   60

    The Fable   63

    The Proverb   70

Fable and Proverb as Exempla of
   the Work of Poetic Art in General   71
Conclusion   75

*Chapter Four: Functional Determination of
              the Work of Poetic Art*   *79*

The Teleology of Poetic Images   79
Cognitive Function   82
Expressive Function   91
Auxiliary Functions   94
Criticism as a Mode of Cognition   97
Conclusion   101

*Chapter Five: Potebnja's Theory: Axiomatic System or
               a Set of Observational Propositions*   *105*

Potebnja versus Potebnjanism   105
Potebnja and the Symbolists   120
The Formalist Response to Potebnja's Theory   124
Potebnja and the Vagaries of Soviet Ideology   128

Conclusion   133
Bibliography   141
Index   161

Introduction

Alexander A. Potebnja's theory of literature is virtually unknown to Western critics. With the exception of one brief précis in René Wellek's *History of Modern Criticism*, another in Victor Erlich's *Russian Formalism*, and an outline in my *Psychologism and Psychoaesthetics*, very little has been written about it. This inattention is not due to a bias against East European criticism—it was caused by Potebnja himself. He did not regard criticism as his main intellectual concern and focused, instead, on linguistics. His publications in literary theory comprise only three works. Only one of the three was his own, formal composition, written while he was a young lecturer at Kharkiv University. The other two were his lecture notes, which were posthumously compiled, edited, and published by his students. The three works are more compendiums of loosely integrated views and citations from Wilhelm Humboldt, Heymann Steinthal, Hermann Lotze, and Moritz Lazarus than systematic inquiries into the issues of literary criticism. Thus Potebnja's literary theory, given more *in ovo* than *in extenso,* must be amplified by, and reconstructed from, the psycholinguistic formulations presented in his works on language, mythology, and folklore.

The reception of Potebnja's theory in the Russian Empire itself was at first constrained. As Erlich commented, the environment was one in which "the view of literature as a mirror of society or preferably as a vehicle for social change, enjoyed a distinct advantage over both the detached psychological curiosity and a systematic concern with the writer's psyche."[1] In time, however, Potebnja's theory became to some scholars and critics the exclusive explanation of poetic art, and to others, a major provocation to construct their own. This keen

---

[1] Victor Erlich, *Russian Formalism: History–Doctrine* (The Hague: Mouton, 1955).

interest was cut short in the early 1930s by Socialist Realism, the official Soviet theory of the creative arts. As O. P. Presnjakov remarked, "from the end of the 1920s and all the way through the 1950s, Potebnja had not been written about. Only his linguistic legacy was substantially elucidated, but even that was [done] through isolated and rare articles."[2] In the 1960s Potebnja's theory again became "the classical inheritance of philological science" in the Soviet Union. This reversal was accompanied by an all-out effort to prove that Potebnja, in spite of "serious errors [that is, his neo-Kantian position], defended the materialistic comprehension of the world," and was, indeed, "a master of dialectical materialism."[3]

In the history of Western critical thought Potebnja's theory stands alongside the theories affected by Wilhelm Humboldt's philosophy of language, particularly those of Benedetto Croce, Karl Vossler, Leo Spitzer, and even Erich Auerbach. For Potebnja, as for these scholars, language and the verbal arts were coterminous phenomena; hence, as Croce observed, "whoever studies general Linguistic, that is to say, philosophical Linguistic, studies aesthetic problems, and *vice versa. Philosophy of language and philosophy of art are the same thing.*"[4] As if anticipating these scholars, Potebnja conceived of poetic art as a perpetual activity that, while creating ever-novel meanings, does not proscribe or deprecate preceding ones. And like these scholars, he ascribed to "representation" or "internal form" the preeminent locus in the structure of poetic art. Without that representation, he held, poetic art is but a communicative or referential cipher with a limited, strictly defined function.

There was, of course, a noteworthy difference between Potebnja and these later scholars. To him, the "internal form" was a linguistic given, identical with the etymon of the word, while to them it was identical with the "aesthetic imagination" (Croce), the "creative principle of the speaking mind" (Vossler), the "life-blood of the

[2] O. P. Presnjakov, *A. A. Potebnja i russkoe literaturovedenie konca XIX – XX veka* (Saratov: Izd. Saratovskogo universiteta, 1978).

[3] D. X. Ostrjanyn, "Filosofs'ke značennja naukovoji spadščyny O. O. Potebni," in *Oleksandr Opanasovyč Potebnja: Juvilejnyj zbirnyk do 125-riččja z dnja narodžennja* ed. M. A. Žovtobrjux et al., (Kiev: AN URSR, 1962), pp. 42 – 45.

[4] Benedetto Croce, *Aesthetic as Science of Expression and General Linguistic* (New York: Noonday Press, 1962), p. 142.

poetic creation" (Spitzer), or other similar, metaphorically-defined entities. Potebnja's linguistic definition of internal form derived from his belief that ethnopsychology imparts to linguistic and poetic codes the final authority of semiosis. To Croce and the others, this thesis was not valid, inasmuch as it prevented these codes from generating meaning outside a particular time and place.

Potebnja's theory continues to command our attention even when compared with current critical thought—especially formal/structural and phenomenological thought. With the former it shares the notion that on the level of empirical reality, the creative arts in general, and the poetic in particular, are but signifying forms or signs that stand *for* something *to* someone *in* some circumstance. This fundamental semiotic notion, similar to one proposed at approximately the same time by Charles Sanders Peirce, was a consequence of Kant's epistemology, to which both adhered. To Potebnja, as indeed to all Kantian theorists of knowledge, poetic texts represented an intentional synthesis, or unity, of the manifold. There was and remains, certainly, a substantive difference between Potebnja, Peirce, and latter-day semioticians. Potebnja firmly believed that the diachronic depth of the signifiers was ethnic and therefore finite, while Peirce conceived of it as infinitely regressive. "The interpretant," Peirce stated, "is nothing but another representation to which the torch of truth is handed along; and as representation, it has its interpretant again. Lo, another infinite series."[5]

On the level of semantic decoding, or what linguists call the level of relations in absentia, Potebnja's theory also stands close to current critical thought. It postulates a perennial asymmetry between the given and the inferred. To him, however, these relations are determined not so much by the specific context or by the differential integers of the statement (as structuralists, for example, have claimed), but by the specific vision of the world encoded in the internal forms of language. This vision translates itself into a distinct semantic concept in regard to both language and the poetic text. In refuting general meanings and upholding polysemy, Potebnja's linguistics and aesthetics anticipated those current theories which conceive of verisimilitude, or indeed truth itself, in terms of discourse/belief rather than in terms

[5] Charles Sanders Peirce, *The Collected Papers of Charles Sanders Peirce,* 8 vols. (Cambridge: Harvard University Press, 1931–1958), 2: 300.

of discourse/referent. In other words, Potebnja believed that the specific vision of the world communicates meaning to reality, whereas de Saussure, for example, believed in the differential combination of signs.

Unlike the structuralists of today, Potebnja insisted on the dynamic role of the Self in the processes of poetic creation and perception. In this respect there is some similarity between him and the phenomenologists, which undoubtedly issued from a common source—Kant's model of the human mind. In the same vein, Potebnja conceived of the Self as an internal eye that sees and knows—without seeing and knowing itself. To the extent, however, that knowledge is predication, and that we do not know the predicates of the Self, the Self remains undefinable. In saying this, Potebnja was not, as some phenomenologists have been, a transcendental subjectivist; rather, he was a critical realist who recognized the interdependence of Self and the outer world. Self to him was a progressively emerging phenomenon, a historical rather than atemporal authentication of man's uniqueness amid everything that constitutes his world. Self may emerge out of the "dark ground" in which there is "total indistinctness between I and non-I,"[6] but in time it arises as the only psychological agency through which that ground reveals itself. The split of this "dark ground" is substantiated through language. As Humboldt, Potebnja's *maître,* observed: "When the soul actually awakens to the feeling that language is not merely a means of exchange for mutual understanding, but a real world, which the spirit must set between itself and objects by an inner exertion of its powers, the soul is on its way to finding more and more in language and to putting more and more into it."[7]

Potebnja's linguistic theory, an ingenious synthesis of Wilhelm Humboldt's philosophy and Heymann Steinthal's psychology of language, is not *l'archéologie du savoir.* Even though its semantics has now been superseded by a more advanced psycholinguistics, the theory's fundamental assertion about the ethnocultural determination of meaning is still very much evident in the works of neo-

---

[6] A. A. Potebnja, "Mysl' i jazyk," in *Èstetika i poètika,* comp. I. V. Ivan'o and A. I. Kolodnaja (Moscow: Iskusstvo, 1976), p. 170.

[7] Cited in Ernst Cassirer, *The Philosophy of Symbolic Forms,* vol. 3 (New Haven and London: Yale University Press 1973), p. 51.

Humboldtian linguistics, particularly in Leo Weisgerber's.[8] Benjamin Whorf, independent of Humboldt's linguistics, has made a similar assertion. When Whorf, quoting Edward Sapir, wrote that the "real world is to a large extent unconsciously built up on the language habits of the group"[9] (which to a great extent we see and hear and otherwise experience as we do because the language habits of our community predispose certain choices of interpretation), he was voicing the ideas Potebnja had formulated half a century earlier. Sapir's distinction between morphemically opaque and morphemically transparent words also reminds us very much of Potebnja's obsolete and living etymological derivatives. Potebnja, in contrast to current ethnolinguistics, whose semantic relativism prevents them from developing a viable theory of cognitive unity, did not extend the concept of the living etymon to all linguistic modalities; therefore he could ascribe universal validity to science and to all forms of advanced cognition. "In science," he wrote, "the only constructing material is concept, made up of the image's objectivized attributes in the word."[10] Scientific abstraction is thus but a suspension of the collective diachrony and the actualization of the differential synchrony. Leo Weisgerber, an avowed ethnolinguist, can say that "linguistic contents (*Sprachinhalte*), even though attached to the sign, are not determined by it."[11] Potebnja could not say this, especially not in regard to scientific language, in which the external forms of the signs are the sole indicators of its referents.

Though Potebnja's theory was neither historically nor synchronically novel in the West, it was wholly new in the Russian Empire. S. Krymskij correctly said that in Russia, Potebnja was "one of the first to put the study of the history of cognition, in conjunction with language, on the ground of factual research, [and the first] to attempt to determine the general semantic principles of man's apprehension of

---

[8] Cf. Leo Weisgerber, "Die sprachliche Erschliessung der Welt," in *Von den Kräften der deutschen Sprache,* vol. 3 (Düsseldorf: Pädagogischer Verlag Schwann, 1953).

[9] Benjamin Lee Whorf, "The Relation of Habitual Thought and Behavior to Language," in *Language, Culture, and Personality: Essays in Memory of Edward Sapir,* ed. L. Spier et al. (Menasha, Wisc.: Sapir Memorial Publ. Fund, 1941), p. 77.

[10] Potebnja, "Mysl' i jazyk," p. 195.

[11] Leo J. Weisgerber, "Die inhaltbezogene Grammatik," *Von den Kräften der deutschen Sprache,* vol. 3 (Düsseldorf: Pädgogischer Verlag Schwann, 1953), p. 81.

the basic categorical relations of reality.''[12] To this one could add that he was the first to define the work of poetic art as a linguistic given whose two planes—expression and content—are, as a rule, asymmetrical. In contrast to Russian theorists who posited images as the principal category of the poetic text, he was the first to infer the triune semantic possibility of the expression/content relationship—mythological, poetic, and scientific. Moreover, he was the first to conceive of these possibilities as concomitant rather than sequential, thus implying their continual coexistence.

* * * * *

Alexander A. Potebnja was born on 22 October, 1835, in the village of Havrylivka in the Kharkiv province of the Ukraine. He graduated from a secondary school in the Polish town of Radom. In 1851 he matriculated at Kharkiv University's faculty of law. Due to a growing interest in folklore and philology, after two years he transferred to the faculty of history and philology. Potebnja completed his studies in 1856 by defending the thesis "The Initial Years of Bohdan Xmel'nyc'kyj's War." Two years later he was appointed lecturer, and, then, upon submitting the master's thesis "Some Symbols in Slavic Poetry," he was named assistant professor of Russian philology at his alma mater.

In 1862 Potebnja published a series of articles on literary theory in a journal of the Ministry of Education. The series soon reappeared in book form as *Mysl' i jazyk* (Thought and Language), a work destined to be republished in five editions. That same year he left for the University of Berlin to further his philological studies. At the news of his brother's tragic death during the Polish uprising in 1863, Potebnja returned to Kharkiv and resumed academic work as a docent of Russian philology. In 1865 his doctoral thesis, "On the Mythological Significance of Some Rituals and Superstitions," was rejected.

Most of the work he published during this period dealt with the phonology and dialectology of East Slavic languages. In 1874 he submitted and successfully defended another doctoral thesis: this time,

[12] S. B. Krymskij, "Potebnja, Aleksandr Afanas'evič," in *Filosofskaja ènciklopedija* ed. F. V. Konstantinov, vol. 4 (Moscow: Sovetskaja ènciklopedija, 1967), p. 327.

the strictly linguistic work *Iz zapisok po russkoj grammatike* (Notes on Russian Grammar), which, in spite of its innocuous title, proved encyclopedic in both thematic scope and depth. On the basis of an enormous quantity of data from practically all the Slavic and Balto-Slavic languages, dialects, and folklores, he addressed the major issues of Slavic morphology and syntax. This monumental work earned him immediate recognition and a secure place in the annals of Slavic philology. He was then promoted to professorial rank, elected corresponding member of the Imperial Academy of Sciences, and awarded the prestigious Lomonosov prize. Along with his research and lectures in linguistics, he also lectured on the theory of literature, on folklore, and on individual writers.

Potebnja died on 11 December, 1891, at the age of fifty-six. His death was noted in obituaries both in the Russian Empire and abroad.[13] In 1894, his wife Maria published, at her own expense, the volume *Iz lekcij po teorii slovesnosti* (Lectures on the Theory of Literature), a compendium of her husband's private lectures delivered to a group of women at their home. In 1904, Maria published *Iz zapisok po teorii slovesnosti* (Notes on the Theory of Literature) which was edited by Potebnja's students V. I. Xarciev, A. V. Vetuxov, B. A. Lezin, and V. I. Kašerinov, who together chose the volume's title.

[13] Cf. "Pamjati A. A. Potebni," in *Sbornik Xar'kovskogo istoričesko-filologičeskogo obščestva* vol. 4, (Kharkiv: 1892), pp. 1–90.

CHAPTER ONE

The Essential Being
of the Work of Poetic Art

Epistemological Constraints

The essential being of the work of poetic art, in the belief of Potebnja and his German mentors Humboldt and Steinthal, is not fully accessible to man's apodictic knowledge. The limitation has a number of reasons and foremost among them are linguistic ones. In attempting to locate and describe that which makes the object what it is, man must inevitably resort to linguistic conceptualization, and thereby to a set of cognitive rules by which the synthetic representation of the object becomes possible. Such representation, regardless of whether it is brought about by understanding or by imagination, is, by virtue of being a linguistic construct, reductive, interpretive, analytic, and so forth, but hardly ever homologous. Hence, Potebnja wrote, "the essential attributes that represent or replace many others are essential only for a particular point of view and not unconditionally. This essentiality is not an expression of the unknown essence of the thing, but a subjective act of the unification of attributes whose real connection is unknown to us."[1]

For Kant, whose theory of cognition is readily recognizable in Potebnja's position, representation (*Vorstellung*) simply meant sense awareness and knowledge. For Potebnja, however, it also meant an experience couched in language. Thus, the unification of the stimulatory input that we receive from this or that object occurs within and through the matrix of language. Cassirer aptly summarized

---

[1] A. A. Potebnja, *Iz zapisok po teorii slovesnosti. Poèzija i proza. Tropy i figury. Myšlenie poètičeskoe i mifičeskoe. Priloženija.* (Kharkiv: M. Zil'berg, 1905; Slavic Printings and Reprints, The Hague: Mouton, 1970), p. 61.

Humboldt's epistemological position: "Man not only thinks the world and understands it through the medium of language, his whole intuition of it and the way in which he lives in this intuition are conditioned by this very medium. His grasp of an objective reality—the way in which he sets it before himself as a whole and forms, divides, and articulates it in particular—none of this would be possible without the living energy of language."[2] At the same time, however, language also restricts man from grasping reality as it actually is. Rather than facilitating direct access to reality, it creates a symbolic correlate to it. Consequently, instead of becoming the direct datum of cognition, the perception of this reality is converted into verbal signs and codes; between man and reality exists a language stratum through which he experiences reality and over which he cannot prevail. This dual nature of language—facilitating and restrictive—renders cognition a highly complex process, involving both the noetic and the orectic dimensions.

Within this definition, Potebnja distinguished languages with different functions and different epistemological possibilities. The language of science and the language of poetry, among others, represent major variable attempts to know reality in its authentic givenness. However, neither of these attempts succeeds fully, since "in a broad as well as a strict sense, all claims of [our] thought, even though determined by the external world, are subjective and therefore the products of personal creativity."[3]

In this far-reaching subjectivism, Potebnja further alleged, we can nevertheless distinguish objective from subjective, and science from art. The principal vehicle of poetic apprehension of reality is the image, while that of science is the concept. "If art is the process of the primary givens of mental life, science is the process of the objectification of art. The difference in the degree of objectivity of thought is equivalent to the difference in the degree of its abstraction."[4] Of all possible languages, mathematics is the most objective:

---

[2] Cassirer, *The Philosophy of Symbolic Forms*, 3: 207.
[3] Potebnja, "Mysl' i jazyk," p. 195.
[4] Ibid.

In its propositions, it is the "most indubitable and the least permissive of the personal viewpoint."[5]

The cognition of the poetic work of art represents an even more formidable task than that of autonomously existing reality, for, as Humboldt observed, its essence "lies not in the nature of its objects but in the mood of the imagination,"[6] or, as we would say today, in the heteronomy of the subject/object relation. An inquiry into such a work inevitably involves self-cognition. The exact parameters of subject/object we cannot establish definitively, because the content of our mind (*duša*) in such cognition is largely unknown to us, while the poetic object in question, once perceived, changes instantaneously. "Something changes," Potebnja wrote, "in the very thought at the time it enters [our] consciousness, but precisely what—it is very unlikely we will ever be able to say, because we would have to know both, and we know only the thought that has transferred into consciousness and has incorporated into itself those properties which it had in the unconscious condition."[7]

What, then, are the epistemological prospects? Humboldt was rather blunt in advocating the personal prerogatives of the conscientious scholar: "So long as he is certain that the artist has operated with all the full and pure powers at his disposal (and in this he must be allowed free and arbitrary judgment), he can do nothing more than take his offspring as it comes, describe it simply, and—if it resists his classification—extend his system in accordance with its need."[8] Potebnja was more cautious. To him critical analysis, with all its limitations, served primarily a heuristic goal. Such an analysis "renders *history* possible, which [in turn] gives and supports the conviction that the world of mankind is subjective; that [this world] is but the shift in world views, the truth of which lies only in their necessity; that we can posit our view as a true one and oppose the previous as false only

---

[5] Ibid.

[6] W. Humboldt, "Über Goethes *Hermann und Dorothea*," in *Gesammelte Schriften,* 17 vols. (Berlin: Königliche Preussische Akademie der Wissenschaften, 1903–1936), 2: 132.

[7] Ibid., p. 128.

[8] Ibid., p. 121.

because we lack the means to verify it."[9] Knowledge, it follows, is relative, while our quest for truth is infinite.

In more practical terms, the cognition of the work of poetic art, Potebnja contends, must be free of all such external and internal impediments as, for example, bias—a ready judgment that we, often involuntarily, impose on the object under study. "Bias," Potebnja wrote, "is what we have decided earlier, and what was correct and right, but what happens to be incorrect with a new turn of our thought."[10] Usually it is part of the deductive inferences or generalizations that we apply uncritically to the fluctuating data of our perception. Therefore, "the general rule . . . even though insufficient for the complete elimination of such biases, is to treat such abstractions merely as a means for our thought, rather than to subject ourselves to them and to look at them as the only source of our knowledge."[11]

Potebnja's remark about external and internal impediments to our cognition is reminiscent of, although considerably less radical than, the *epoché* of Descartes or Husserl. He, unlike them, was a relativist in epistemology.

The Work of Poetic Art as Activity

Roman Ingarden, in his ontological investigation of reality, proposed a taxonomy of the object on the basis of its existential moment (*momentum existentiae*) and existential modality (*modus existentiae*), rather than on the basis of its existence as an abstract idea. Such a system of classification shifts our attention from abstract reasoning to phenomena directly perceived and directly experienced. Ontological inquiry could, as a result, address the problem of existence as it occurs in the real world, without sacrificing eidetic analysis. Potebnja's definition of creative arts as "activity" (*dejatel'nost'*), becomes defensible within the strictures of such a taxonomy.

What then, in Potebnja's view, is the existential mode of the work of poetic art? Existing as an imaginative representation (*predstavlenie*) of the actual, plausible, probable, and impossible realities, it

---

[9] Potebnja, *Iz zapisok po teorii slovesnosti*, p. 408.
[10] Potebnja , "Iz lekcij po teorii slovesnosti," *Èstetika i poètika*, p. 465.
[11] Potebnja, "Iz lekcij po teorii slovesnosti," p. 465.

is an activity intended to elicit varied knowledge about these realities. It is a form of syntactic predication whose function is to bring about certain cognitive dispositions in the person initiating it as well as in the person perceiving it. Like linguistic predication in general, the work of art is *energeia,* a perpetually created construct, rather than a completed artifact, or *ergon.*

Activity, as a general category that subsumes most of man's behavior, is, or can be, directed on the one hand toward production (transformation, adaptation, and destruction of such objects as food, clothing and habitat, as well as everything that indirectly relates to them—such as conveyances, hunting, war, and so forth); and, on the other hand, predominantly toward transformation of production itself. Hypothetically, activity can be of either a practical or of a theoretical nature, but it is usually a synthesis of the two, because exclusive practicality or exclusive theory may attenuate its significance. Even the explicitly theoretical activity that seems to have nothing to do with the production of material substances is practical, in the sense that it transforms its producer. Practical activity, likewise, in order to sustain its direction must be grounded in theory. Practical activity yields handicraft; theoretical activity yields science, scholarship, and art.

This pragmatic division of activity has a psychophysical justification. Handicraft, Potebnja asserted,[12] employs both the lower senses (such as common sense [*obščee čuvstvo,*] touch, taste, and fascination) and the higher ones (such as seeing and hearing).[13] Science, which includes scholarship and art, involves only seeing and hearing, because the impressions of the lower senses are transmitted to the higher ones by means of language. According to this same justification, theoretical activity is split into three subsets: one contingent upon seeing (architecture, sculpture, painting, and mime), one contingent upon seeing and hearing (dance accompanied by music), and one contingent only upon hearing (music, poetry, and science).

[12] Potebnja, *Iz zapisok po teorii slovesnosti,* p. 2.

[13] Potebnja's classification of sensory perception into lower and higher had been taken from J. F. Herbart's *Psychologie als Wissenschaft.*

Human Activity

Practical		*Theoretical*	
various handicrafts	*seeing*	*seeing-hearing*	*hearing*
	architecture	dance w/music	music
	sculpture		poetry
	painting, mime		science

Works of practical activity and of the first subset of the theoretical are analogous in that they deal with and alter material extraneous to the producer. Upon completion, these works remain fixed and need no reproduction, unlike the works of the remaining subsets, which must be reproduced each time they are to be perceived. "Every time they are perceived," Potebnja wrote, "they are born anew. The visible signs through which they are affirmed are merely the means of their reproduction, rather than their true existence."[14] In this sense they are pure activities.

Works of theoretical activity are further divisable into spatial and temporal categories. Architecture, sculpture, and painting—the spatial arts—differ from music and poetry in that they "depict one moment, containing in itself the variety of perceptions"[15]—that is, they present the intended object aspectually. Presentation of movement is virtually impossible for them, while the temporal arts represent nothing but movement. In them the visual perceptions (mime, dance) and audio perceptions (music, poetry) form a series, a chain whose links retreat into the past and remain in the memory as the succeeding ones occur.[16]

The consequences of such a division were obvious to Potebnja. Citing a widely known thesis of Gotthold Lessing (*Laokoon*, 1766), he stated that "signs situated one after another should depict only such objects or their parts as in reality appear in the temporal sequence."[17]

---

[14] Potebnja, *Iz zapisok po teorii slovesnosti*, p. 13.

[15] Ibid., p. 4.

[16] Ibid., p. 5.

[17] Ibid., p. 6. Potebnja was not alone in adopting Lessing's definition of simultaneous and successive arts. In fact, the German aestheticians of the second half of the nineteenth century—Zeisling, Vischer, Gerber, Schasler, Hartmann, and others—all adopted this definition in their incessant classification of the arts. Potebnja was openly critical of other of Lessing's claims (e.g., his definition of fable), writing: "This is being said by a thoughtful man, and therefore his research is important to us,

Disregard for this principle leads to the intrusion of spatial art into temporal art, or vice versa: for example, when Titian depicts the entire story of the prodigal son, presenting different episodes, he invades poetry. In short, spatial relations ought not to be replaced by temporal sequences, because such a substitution impedes the reconstruction of the simultaneously existing whole. The substitution can, however, be made in science (*nauka*), which operates mainly with abstract concepts and therefore demands little imagination from the reader.

The Work of Poetic Art as Narration

"All modes of verbal poetic and prosaic rendition," Potebnja wrote, "are reducible to one thing—narration—since this converts a series of simultaneous signs into a series of successive percepts, into a representation of the movement of vision and thought from object to object.... In speech, the description (that is, the depiction of attributes that exist in space simultaneously) is possible only to the extent that it is converted into narration—the depiction of the sequence of percepts."[18]

This definition of the poetic text as a semiotic correlate of the temporal sequence of percepts has a number of important implications. In a general sense, it implies that textual objects, prior to their transformation into verbal correlates, exist as complete wholes, that is, as real or fictive spatial phenomena. In order to become objects for a subject, however, they must be reduced to representative attributes and thus be converted into a syntactic arrangement, or utterance. As complete wholes, they can be represented only conceptually or algorithmically.

Another implication is that narration, whereby spatial simultaneity becomes temporal sequence, is determined by the very organization of our perceptive and cognitive apparatus. This process, then, is the mode of our sense perception and of our cognition. Man narrates tangible reality sequentially because he perceives it sequentially. By his

---

but a man of the eighteenth century, and (therefore) we cannot agree with him in certain cases." *Iz lekcij po teorii slovesnosti. Basnja, poslovica, pogovorka* (Kharkiv: K. Sčasin, 1894; Slavic Printings and Reprints, 150; The Hague: Mouton, 1970), p. 494.

[18] Ibid., p. 5.

visa and *audita* he encounters only reality's aspects and never its totalities. Such totalities are therefore pure abstractions, myth, or fiction. Natural language records reality for us only attributively or imaginatively. Even logical reflection or reasoning, whose language is ideally free from attributive denotation, organizes its signs and codes as a narrative sequence. "Reasoning," Potebnja observed, "is narration about a consecutive series of thoughts that leads to a certain conclusion."[19] Scientific language, by utilizing logical concepts ("simultaneous aggregates of attributes")[20] is nevertheless fiction.

In sum, narration in the form of poetic language reconstructs or creates sequentially total configurations of spatial simultaneities. To reach what Humboldt called the "independent establishment by summarization,"[21] narration must comply with grammatical rules of the particular language. These rules, unlike universally valid logical rules, are ethnically bound and therefore restricted in application. "The grammatical sentence," Potebnja wrote, "is not at all identical to and parallel with logical judgment."[22] In the former subject and predicate, for example, retain their specific grammatical function, while in the latter, they may be interchanged. A grammatical sentence that precedes the idea (*ponjatie*) secures its existential justification deep in ethnic consciousness rather than in universally valid inferences. Within the structures of this consciousness, such a sentence, even if logically incongruous, might be perfectly appropriate and significative.[23]

Each particular language creates, then, its own narrative structures through which and by which man relates to his existential realities. These structures, like grammatical sentences, might (but not necessarily should) depend upon logical universals. Humboldt describes this intermediary structure: "Thus, from this cosmos reflected in man, originates between him and it . . . that language which associates him

---

[19] Ibid.

[20] Potebnja, "Mysl' i jazyk," p. 166.

[21] W. Humboldt, *Linguistic Variability and Intellectual Development*, trans. G. C. Buck and F. A. Raven (Coral Gables, Florida: University of Miami Press, 1971), p. 163.

[22] Potebnja, *Iz zapisok po russkoj grammatike*, vol. 1 (Kharkiv: Knižnyj magazin D. N. Poluextova, 1888), p. 61.

[23] Ibid., pp. 60–63.

with his environment and which, through his effort, reacts fruitfully upon the latter."[24] The world is subject to a continuous structuralization of man's linguistic activity. This intermediary stratum, which exists as an actual or potential narrative construct, is not, however, identical with the reality it represents or symbolizes. To cite Humboldt again: "Synthesis creates something that is not present per se in any associated constituents."[25] Prose or poetry, Humboldt observed, "moves from reality toward something that does not belong to reality. Poetry conceives of reality in its sensuous phenomenality, as it is externally and internally perceived by us. . . . It relates the sensuous phenomena in the creative imagination, and through them guides us to a view of an artistically ideal wholeness."[26]

The Work of Poetic Art as Teleologically Charged Form

If the essence of the work of poetic art is *energeia*—activity and mobility—can it be said to have fixed forms? Would not such constancy be, to use Humboldt's expression, an "incomplete mummified depository,"[27] or *ergon*? The *energeia* of the work of poetic art, in order to be something, expresses itself through spatial and temporal relations or, as Kant put it, attaches itself to the categories of time and space and thus begins to operate in a constant and uniform manner. Through these categories it assumes fixed form.

Humboldt and Potebnja believed that the appearance of form is inconceivable without human spirit (or more specifically, without national spirit), but they differed on the nature of this spirit. To Humboldt, as to Hegel, spirit permeates man's consciousness through the medium of language and compels it to form, as well as to destroy, physical and symbolic realities. This spirit, even though coterminous with language, is nevertheless transcendant to it. "The truly creative

---

[24] Humboldt, *Linguistic Variability,* p. 163.

[25] Ibid., p. 67.

[26] W. Humboldt, "Über die Verschiedenheit des menschlichen Sprachbaues und ihren Einfluss auf die geistige Entwicklung des Menschengeschlechts," in *Gesammelte Schriften,* 7: 193.

[27] Ibid., p. 45.

principle," Humboldt wrote, "operating in the recondite and secret course of mankind's development, is the power of the intellect (*Geist*) which sallies forth from its inner depth and plenitude to intervene in events of the world."[28] Potebnja rejected this essentially metaphysical view of spirit and attempted to define it psychologically. By identifying language with spirit, he stated, Humboldt "blocks the way toward any further research."[29] Spirit, in Potebnja's view, is a "conscious intellectual activity"[30] that presupposes ideas. These, in turn, are rendered by language. In this restricted sense, language and spirit are contingent phenomena. "Spirit is impossible without language because it is being created by it, and language for it [spirit] is its initial event."[31] As a result, the synchrony of spirit and language occurs at the time when ideas can be and are generated by words. However, on the level of pure abstraction (for example, in some sciences), "conscious intellectual activity" might function without natural language—through purely arbitrary signs.

In regard to the issue of constant forms, Potebnja maintained, first, that they are created within the matrices of linguistically homogeneous collectives; second, that the relationship between the spirit and these forms (or between *energeia* and *ergon*) is dialectical and hence neither of them is primary; third, that these forms may turn into a "mummified depository" if they lose the capacity for dynamic representation; and finally, that being phenomena of the human mind, they are relative rather than absolute, as Humboldt alleged. Both scholars agree that linguistic and poetic forms represent the "individuated urge by means of which a nation creates validity in language for its thoughts and feelings."[32]

As a linguistic given, the work of poetic art is identical with its formal modality. It cannot be separated, extrapolated, or abstracted from it; its formal structure subsumes its being. The reality that this work refers or alludes to, likewise, cannot be separated from its linguistic rendition, because, to use Humboldt's apt expression, it appears to man through the sensuous vividness of his language. Poetic art

---

[28] Humboldt, *Linguistic Variability*, p. 7.
[29] Potebnja, "Mysl' i jazyk," p. 67.
[30] Ibid., p. 69.
[31] Ibid.
[32] Humboldt, "Über die Verschiedenheit," p. 47.

"never treats an object as isolated and never uses the sum total of its reality. It always skims off its surface relationships, condition, points of view, and combines these."[33] This correlative dependence of language and reference is less true of purely referential and scientific texts, in which semiosis and signification are not necessarily contingent upon exclusive rendition. In poetic texts, Potebnja stated, reality is represented exclusively, or as Humboldt said, as the texts constitute themselves externally and internally.

The formal modality of the work of poetic art is crucial, therefore, for both its taxonomy and ontology, because it determines the work's existential distinction. At the same time, it would be a mistake to consider this modality the sole antecedent of the work's being, as, for example, the formalist school did. While it is true that "there can be no unformed substance—no raw materiality,"[34] it is equally true that in symbolic reality this substance is constituted not only in terms of the posited form, but also in terms of the aesthetic addenda provided by the apperceiving consciousness. In spite of its restricted role, the formal modality of the work of poetic art has particular importance, because it is imbued with intentionality directed toward a certain goal: the expression of thought. In other words, it is a telic construct.

By analogy with the natural language, in which external and internal forms arouse specific cognitive acts, Potebnja inferred that the specific modality of the work of poetic art is simultaneously linked with a corresponding apperceptive process. Here, like Humboldt before him,[35] Potebnja insisted on the principle of semantic simultaneity. This was a radical departure from the position widely shared by rationalists, according to which thinking and speaking were distinct activities, and language was thereby thought to be a strictly auxiliary phenomenon. Thought and language, according to Humboldt and Potebnja, are simultaneous acts and therefore do not and cannot exist

---

[33] W. Humboldt, "Latium und Hellas oder Betrachtungen über das klassische Alterthum," in *Gesammelte Schriften,* 3: 170.

[34] Humboldt, "Über die Verschiedenheit," p. 46.

[35] W. Humboldt, "Lettre à Abel-Remusat sur la nature des formes grammaticales en général et sur le genie de la langue chinoise en particulier," *Journal Asiatique* 9 (1826): 115.

separately.[36] Potebnja observed: "If we recognize our thought by the word, then for us (and not only for the listener) it comes into being and changes together with its verbal expression."[37]

In science, a split between the signifier and signified is possible by the very fact that the latter may exist in multiple denotations. Potebnja explains this possibility by the substantive difference between imaginative and conceptual languages. In the former, the connection between image and idea is apprehended intuitively, at once, and need not be proven. In the latter, the inclusion of facts into existing axioms must be demonstrated, for science allegedly consists of nothing but such axioms. Scientific proof, Potebnja observed, is tantamount to a systematic decomposition of elementary data. Thus, it may be rendered by different, though related, signs. Poetic images cannot. Aesthetic forms, external and internal, are therefore creations *sui generis*.

The Word as an Analogue of the Work of Poetic Art

Jurij Tynjanov, a leading Russian formalist, observed: "The grandiose attempt made by Potebnja to construct a theory of literature ranging from the word as ἕν to a complex literary work as πᾶν was doomed to fail, for the essence of the relationship of ἕν to πᾶν lies in the heterogeneity and varied functional significance of this ἕν. The concept of 'material' does not exceed the boundaries of form, being itself formal. It is a mistake to confuse this concept with extraconstructive properties."[38] This astute observation is as accurate as it is misleading. While more will be said about Potebnja's position on the structural analogy between the two, it is necessary, in order to complete Potebnja's view of the essential being of the work of poetic art, to define this analogy in general terms.

---

[36] Before Humboldt, the "concept of simultaneity" was shared by a host of scholars, among them S. G. Hamann (1730–1788) and J. G. Herder (1744–1803).

[37] Potebnja, *Iz zapisok po russkoj grammatike*, 3:8.

[38] Jurij Tynjanov, "Rhythm as the Constructive Factor of Verse," in *Readings in Russian Poetics: Formalist and Structuralist Views,* ed. Ladislav Matejka and Krystyna Pomorska (Cambridge: MIT Press, 1971), p. 126.

Tynjanov is indeed correct about Potebnja's intention to disclose the affinites between the word and the work of poetic art and to construct his poetics on this basis. As Ivan'o and Kolodnaja accurately stated, Potebnja's

> point of departure in regard to art's concepts was the thought about the analogy of structures of the word and the work of art. . . . This constant analogy, "word-work of art," plays an important methodological role in his theory. Potebnja frequently stresses the fact that language as a whole and the word in particular correspond to art not only by the elements of their combination. Art is the same type of activity as language, differing from it only in that it is more conscious. The basic components of art are image and signification; its language is polysemous; the secret of its poeticalness lies in the fact that the image is less than the signification, and the specificity of art is based on the disproportion of the number of images and the multitude of possible significations.[39]

On the other hand, Tynjanov is wrong when he implies that Potebnja does not perceive the varied functional significance of the word, and that Potebnja posits a dichotomy of "material" and "form" in the work of poetic art.

Humboldt and Potebnja conceived of language as a medium through which we both understand and create our world.[40] Language, consequently, does not merely provide a phonetic designation of the perceived objects; it forms them. Language and perceived objects are thus inseparable.[41]

---

[39] I. V. Ivan'o and A. I. Kolodnaja, "Èstetičeskaja koncepcija A. Potebni," in Potebnja, *Èstetika i poètika,* p. 16.

[40] At the same time, Humboldt observed that man "senses and knows that language is only a means for him; that there is an invisible realm outside in which he seeks to feel at home; and that it is for this reason that he needs the aid of language. The most common observation and the profoundest thought both lament the inadequacy of language. Both look upon that other realm as a distant country toward which only language leads—and it never really arrives. All higher forms of speech are wrestling with this thought in which sometimes our power, sometimes our longing, is more keenly felt." "Über den Nationalcharakter der Sprachen," in *Gesammelte Schriften,* 4: 434.

[41] In a debate with the philologist and folklorist F. I. Buslaev (1818–1897), Potebnja argued that what Buslaev called matter, or the content of the sentence, was in fact nothing but form. He wrote: "Recognizing that even what Buslaev calls matter

Deeming this view of language almost axiomatic, Potebnja could not but treat the work of poetic art as an organic whole that tolerates no division into form and material. As a directly observable and palpable given, it has only external and internal forms, only articulated sounds and complimentary images. The intended reality or objects are given partially or attributively rather than fully; the internal form only invokes a corresponding reference in the perceiving consciousness. The point is not whether the image or some definite idea corresponds, but whether this image is infinitely capable of corresponding to ever-new ideas, of invoking and begetting ever-new thoughts, of explaining the infinite series of life's phenomena. For all this to become concrete, the text needs to be responded to by the reader, or as Mixail Baxtin observed decades after Potebnja, the text needs to be dialogized.[42] Humboldt also was very explicit about this point: "All speaking is founded on dialogue (*Wechselrede*) in which, even when more than two are present, the speaker always opposes the ones spoken to as a unit other than himself. Even in his thoughts, man speaks to an 'other' or to himself as though he were an 'other' and draws his circles of spiritual relationships accordingly, separating those who speak 'his language' from those who do not."[43] Potebnja expressed a similar idea: "Speech is indivisible from understanding; and the speaker who, even though he might feel that the word belongs to him, presupposes at the same time that the word and representation do not constitute his

---

is not matter but a 'manner of combination,' we shall alter his position this way: In every sentence we should distinguish form and form; in the sentence there is nothing but form. Thus if we were to deprive it of its form, we would destroy the sentence of the inflectional languages." *Iz zapisok po russkoj grammatike,* 1:65.

[42] In the glossary of the key concepts in Baxtin's theory, Michael Holquist summarized dialogism this way: "Dialogism is the characteristic epistemological mode of a world dominated by heteroglossia. Everything means, is understood, as a part of a greater whole—there is a constant interaction between meanings, all of which have the potential of conditioning others. Which will affect the other, how it will do so and in what degree is what is actually settled at the moment of utterance. This dialogic imperative mandated by the pre-existence of the language world relative to any of its current inhabitants, insures that there can be no actual monologue." M. Bakhtin, *The Dialogic Imagination,* ed. Michael Holquist (Austin: University of Texas Press, 1981), p. 426.

[43] Humboldt, "Über den Dualis," in *Gesammelte Schriften,* 6:25.

exclusive and personal property, because what he understands also belongs to the listener."[44]

Potebnja was acutely aware of the "varied functional significance of the ἕν if by ἕν we understand the word in general. The word— depending upon the nature of its internal form and its syntactic environment—may function poetically, prosaically, referentially, emotively, expressively, or merely phonetically. Although Potebnja did not define these functions as specifically as the Russian formalists did, his two categories—poetic and prosaic—do imply them.

The word, in Potebnja's view, does not function poetically under all circumstances. While initially it might have been the manifest symbol of all the properties of the work of art, in time it might become merely a communicative sign. Such a progression from imaginative representation to referential designation is due to the word's semantic expansion and to the corresponding decrease of its imaginative quality. The reverse process, of course, also holds. Language is not, then, a unilinear progression from words to signs or from poetry to prose,[45] but a continuous oscillation between the two. Imaginative presentation and conceptual abstraction are an ever-present possibility of both the poetic and scientific languages.

All this is equally true of the work of poetic art. At first its poeticalness is grounded in the imaginative quality of its language. In time, however, this quality may be exhausted, and the work may thereby cease to be poetical. To Potebnja (contrary to Tynjanov and his fellow formalists), the imaginative quality of the poetic text is not merely a device to construct poetic texts. It is the very essence of the work of poetic art.[46]

From the perspective of phenomenological aesthetics, Potebnja's definition of the work of poetic art lends itself to the following amplification: The work of poetic art is a contingent object, which in

[44] Potebnja, "Mysl' i jazyk," p. 172.

[45] By prose, Potebnja meant also scholarship and science (*nauka*): "We consider prose to be scholarship, even though the two concepts are not always identical. In scholarship the characteristics of the prosaic attitude of mind, which insists on the prosaic form, achieve full determination and contrast to poetry." "Mysl' i jazyk," p. 193.

[46] Victor Shklovsky, "Art as Technique," in *Russian Formalist Criticism: Four Essays,* trans. Lee Lemon and Marion Reis (Lincoln, Neb.: University of Nebraska Press, 1965), p. 7.

order to be must be perceived or must be aesthetically concretized; therefore, its existence is heteronomous rather than autonomous. It subsists rather than exists. As a directly observable given, it contains only two constituents—an external form and an internal form. A third constituent—significance, content, or idea—is attributed to it by the imaginative perception or apperception. This apperception, however, engenders various possibilities for the qualities and relations of the given forms. Their constancy is thus continuously challenged by ever-expanding and changing semantic possibilities. Designating the internal form or image as *A* and its signification as *X,* Potebnja observed: "*X* changes markedly in every new perception of *A* by one and the same person, and even more by another; in the meantime, *A* is the only objective given in the work of poetic art and in perception remains almost unaltered. In contrast to law and fact, the image in poetry is fixed, while its *signification* changes and is defined separately in each case. In a series of cases it is infinite."[47]

To continue with the phenomenological amplification of Potebnja's position, the work of poetic art subsists as a temporal process with a manifest beginning and end. As such, it can be perceived only serially. As a whole it can be reconstructed through a generalizing abstraction, such as synthesis, reduction, paraphrase, evaluation, and the like. Inasmuch, however, as such a whole is usually rendered by different linguistic forms, it is, to quote Humboldt, a "circumlocution for the inexpressible."[48] The whole, as an aesthetic experience, infiltrates all images of the narrative process. It is neither arrested at only some of its semantic focal points nor concentrated at the conclusion of the process itself.

The Conceptual Ambivalence
of Potebnja's Ontology

Potebnja's ontology of the work of poetic art oscillates between romantic transcendentalism, which he inherited from his German mentors, and psychological realism, which was dictated by his linguis-

---

[47] Potebnja, *Iz zapisok po teorii slovesnosti,* p. 101.

[48] Humboldt, "Rezension von Goethes *Zweiter römischer Aufenthalt,*" in *Gesammelte Schriften,* 6: 545.

tic research. His attentiveness to such categories as spirit, imagination, infinity, intuition, and so forth (phenomena that transcend verifiable reality), attests to his romantic judgments, while his systematic concern with such issues as the psychological locus of the work of poetic art, its structure, multimodal function, and value underscore his commitment to realism. This ambivalence in Potebnja's ontology clearly corresponds to the European intellectual atmosphere of the second half of the nineteenth century, when romantic transcendentalism was both fused with and challenged by the empirical sciences, particularly by psychology. Three examples illustrate Potebnja's ambivalent position: his views on the epistemology of the work of poetic art, its essential being as activity or *energeia,* and its uniqueness within the restraining context of the collective consciousness.

In attempting to determine the nature of art, Potebnja came to believe that its activity or function constitutes its entirety. The very moment it ceases to do what it does, it becomes but another static object, an *ergon.* This essentially Aristotelian definition of *existence in actuality* posed a formidable epistemological problem for Potebnja, both in his linguistics and in his aesthetics, because it tended to cloud the specific importance of the agent and the consequence of linguistic and artistic activity. Any determination of activity without a concern for antecedent and subsequent conditions poses the threat of an epistemological impasse, a *petitio principii,* or a romantic esoterism. To say, as Humboldt and Potebnja did, that poetic art was nothing but *energeia* was to dissociate it from the material medium and space, and thus to conceive of it only in terms of an abstract kinesis. At the same time, such an option clearly dictated the actuality of *ens mobile* (or in their terminology, *ergon*), because no motion was conceivable without an object generating it. Obviously, it was for this same reason that while defining the work of poetic art as *energeia,* that is, as quest, activity, and movement in process, both Humboldt and Potebnja found themselves unable to specify its nature. They had no choice but to plead ignorance. "The artist," wrote Humboldt, "does not understand, and the critic can never explain" this process.[49]

---

[49] Humboldt, "Über Goethes *Hermann und Dorothea,*" p. 132.

Logically, Potebnja's emphasis upon *energeia* should have led him to a deemphasis of all tangible forms in artistic creativity, as it did, for Benedetto Croce,[50] a disciple of Humboldt. But it did not. Along with this essentially romantic concept, Humboldt and Potebnja insisted on the formal configuration of artistic creativity, though with a qualification. Humboldt observed: "The creative powers of man—imagination, reason, and feeling—are adapted exclusively to accomplish the transition from finiteness to infinity, which is always an ideal. These powers, in turn, adapt certain forms for their own use, which accept only enough materiality to remain sensuous. They stand in precise relationship to archetypal ideas and, despite being therefore totally definable, always create the impression that their definitude is not a restriction."[51]

Potebnja's simultaneous insistence both on the uniqueness of the work of poetic art and on its contingence upon collective, or ethnic, consciousness was also ambivalent, but of course he was not alone in this. German scholarship of the romantic period, from which he had inherited his key concepts, abounds with this same vacillation, espousing the two disparate contentions in language and poetic art with varying persuasion and empirical evidence. Separately, these contentions might have a high degree of plausibility; together, however, they are ostensibly antinomic, because originality is diametrically opposed to creation according to preexisting modes and rules. Potebnja resolved this dilemma by maintaining that the creation of a work of poetic art does indeed abide by the prevailing linguistic and aesthetic rules, for

---

[50] Croce was aware of this conceptual ambivalence in Humboldt's position: "But Humboldt opposes Humboldt: amongst the old dross we detect the brilliant gleams of a wholly new concept of language. . . . The new man in Humboldt criticizes the old man when he says, 'Languages must be considered not as dead products but as an act of production. . . . Language in its reality is something continuously changing and passing away. Even its preservation in writing is incomplete, a kind of mummification; it is always necessary to render the living speech sensible. Language is not a work, *ergon,* but an activity, *energeia,* . . . It is an eternally repeated effort of the spirit in order to make articulated tones capable of expressing thought.' . . . The new man leads Humboldt to discover a fact hidden from the authors of logico-universal grammars: namely, the internal form of language (innere Sprachform), which is neither logical concept nor physical sound, but the subjective view of things formed by man, the product of imagination and feeling, the individualization of this concept." Croce, *Aesthetic as Science,* p. 327.

[51] Humboldt, "Latium und Hellas," p. 140.

they cannot be radically transcended without rendering inoperative the linguistic matrix. Hence, infinite signification—the sense that the work of poetic art is capable of generating—occurs within a finite grammatical structure. Within this structure, as Humboldt put it, the laws of generation are constant, but the extent and, in a sense, the kind of product remain wholly indefinite. Potebnja expressed a similar idea: "To persons speaking and understanding the same language, the content of a given word is different while its representation is so similar that to the researcher it may appear identical. One can say that the speakers of the same language consider the word's different content from the same point of view."[52] In brief, constancy of form, external and internal, does not necessarily impede polysemy; accordingly, the uniqueness of the work occurs within a commonly shared structure.

From the standpoint of this definition, the work of poetic art does not have to be radically novel in its appearance to function as an original construct. In fact, to generate signification, it must remain within the recognizable rules of construction. Its novelty, indeed its originality, lies "in a certain flexibility of [its] imagery, in the power of [its] internal form to arouse the most varied contents."[53] The uniqueness of the work of poetic art, it follows, is determined by the "infinite (new) determination of the once-formed material."[54] Uniqueness to Potebnja is not that which occurs only once or which differs notably from other creations. The unique work might be and usually is a member of a class, but, unlike other works, it contains "a living embryo of infinite definability."[55] Potebnja did not elaborate why one work contains such an embryo and another does not.

Conclusion

Seen from the perspective of the current discussion of the work of poetic art, Potebnja's ontology stands in proximity to that of phenomenological theory. Like the latter, it locates the being of such a work in the heteronomy of the subject/object homology rather than

---

[52] Potebnja, "Jazyk i narodnost'," in *Èstetika i poètika,* p. 263.
[53] Potebnja, "Mysl' i jazyk," p. 181.
[54] Ibid., p. 189.
[55] Ibid., p. 180.

solely in the work's verifiable expressions or in the subjective experiences generated by them. The coming into being of the work of poetic art is contingent upon the aesthetic concretization of the perceiving subject. This mode of existence—or better, its subsistence—renders the essential being of this work perennially protean. In its ever-new becoming, it realizes its aesthetic and semantic potentialities. These potentialities are not, however, infinite; they persist as long as the work's internal form, "that modality by which its content is being expressed,"[56] retains its imaginative palpability. With its expiration, the work of poetic art turns prosaic. Its structure is thereby reduced to two constituents—external form and signification—and its potential polysemy to a referential monosemy. Such a transformation of poetry into prose is by no means final; the process might also work in reverse. The lost aesthetic vitality of the work's internal form may again be restored.

The work's affirmation by perceptible signs is only the means for its reproduction rather than its true existence. As a formally organized given, it is a verbal construct that realizes itself as it is being perceived. Its goal "is achieved simultaneously with its creation," and therefore "the categories of its goal and its means . . . cannot be differentiated."[57] Any change in its formal structure entails a corresponding change in its teleology; consequently, its goal neither precedes nor follows its form, but is created or recreated simultaneously with it. This temporal symmetry, however, should not be understood as a constancy of form and signification: these are always asymmetrical.

The linkage between poetic form and its semantic intent has an important ontological implication—that the work of poetic art exists only, to use Husserl's term, in *presentification,* within an "extended now," which has a before and an after, and in which whatever existed *in potentia* comes into its full realization. It implies further that with a flow of consciousness, this determined configuration passes over into an ever-fresh retention and there, progressively, is reduced to a functional component in the syntactical concatenation. The question, then, of where and when the work of poetic art is fully realized in Potebnja's theory becomes a crucial one. Although his theory does

<hr/>

[56] Ibid., p. 175.
[57] Potebnja, *Iz zapisok po teorii slovesnosti,* p. 4.

not address this question directly, by reflecting upon the nature of the word as a homologue to the work of poetic art, it does imply an answer. Like the word, the work of poetic art comes into being when its two forms—external and internal—are internalized by our consciousness, or, in Potebnja's terminology, when they are apperceived (when the partial representation of the intended object is explained by data already present in the perceiving mind). Prior to apperception, it exists only as a reference, or as an X, which outside of judgment (*suždenie*) has no sense. For the poetic work to acquire sense and thus to become a fully constituted work of art, it needs man's interpreting consciousness. In short, the work of poetic art exists serially as it is apprehended by our consciousness; however, upon completion of this apprehension, its totality is never the summation of all possible values of X, but rather a reduction of the series either to a few central ideas or to a few prevailing images. As a sum total of all of its imaginative representations, the work of poetic art remains "outside of judgment."

CHAPTER TWO

The Structure of the Work
of Poetic Art

Structural Affinities between Language
and the Work of Poetic Art

In his most acclaimed work on literary theory, *Mysl' i jazyk* (Thought and Language), Potebnja wrote: "Evidently the symbolism of language may be called its poetry (*poètičnost'*), while the oblivion of the internal form seems to us to be the prose (*prozaičnost'*) of the word. Should this comparison be true, then the question of a change of the word's internal form will turn out to be identical with the question of the relationship of language to both poetry and prose—with literary form in general."[1]

From this assumption it was only logical for Potebnja to infer that an inquiry into the language's (or the word's) structure was simultaneously an inquiry into the structure of the poetic work. What, then, is the word? As an articulated sound, derived from the depth of human nature or, as Humboldt said, "as an eternally repeated work of the mind, it enables the thought to express itself."[2] By rendering sensory percepts verbally, it situates them within the collectively held system of reality; it develops and transforms images of the perceived objects into corresponding concepts; it creates new thoughts and either expands or condenses the existing ones. Potebnja wrote metaphorically: "If we compare the creation of thought to the making of cloth,

---

[1] Potebnja, "Mysl' i jazyk," p. 174.

[2] Humboldt, "Über die Verschiedenheit," p. 46. Likewise, Humboldt wrote that "language, as the sum total of its creation, is in each case different from what is uttered." Language "can persist only in a brief span of each thought process, but in its totality it is independent of the process." Idem, *Linguistic Variability,* p. 41.

then the word will be a weaver's shuttle that introduces the weft into
the base threads as well as takes over the slow weaving."[3]

The word, therefore, is more than either merely the minimum unit
or distinctive sound feature of language (as Bloomfield defined it) or a
different linguistic integer in need of syntactic connection (as de Saussure held). Rather, it is a homogeneous semiological act, complete in
both morphology and syntax. Humboldt compared it to the "complete flower bursting from the bud to which the complete product of
language belongs."[4] Possessing the "property of self-significance
(*Selbstbedeutung*), it is necessarily analogous to language as a
whole."[5]

As an act of speech, the word is to be discerned from language—
from the collectively shared system of morphological relations that
regulate all semantically intended verbal constructs. Potebnja contended, much earlier than de Saussure and in explicitly psychological
terms, that "speech ... exists only as part of a larger whole—
language—and [that] in order to comprehend speech one needs to
have present in his mind (*duša*) the multiple relations between the
phenomena given in this speech and those which at the moment of the
speech [*performance*] remain, so to speak, beyond the threshold of
consciousness."[6] This system of relations possesses the flexibility to
receive everything and, in turn, to lend expression to everything. It is
the "building block of thought,"[7] a living creativity, which at every
moment of our speech directs its performance.

For Potebnja the word—speech—consisted of three parts: external
form (the articulated sound), internal form (the modality by which the
word's content is transmitted), and content (idea).[8]

External form, while indivisible from the internal one, is nevertheless distinct from it. As a constituent of the word's triune structure, it
points to a particular signification, not by its synchronic givenness, but

---

[3] Potebnja, "Mysl' i jazyk," p. 167.

[4] Humboldt, *Linguistic Variability*, p. 50.

[5] Ibid., p. 39.

[6] Potebnja, *Iz zapisok po russkoj grammatike*, 1: 34.

[7] Humboldt, "Über die Verschiedenheit," p. 53.

[8] Potebnja refers to these as moments (*momenty*), aspects (*vidy*), and elements
(*stixija*).

"because previously it pointed to a different signification."[9] Thus, for example, the word *versta* (*verst,* equaling 3,500 feet) is used as a measure of distance because formerly it referred to the furrow, which in turn referred to the "turn of the plow," and so on, until, consciously or unconsciously, we are no longer able to determine the diachronic series which is encoded in the collective memory of each linguistically homogeneous community. Hence, Potebnja observed, the articulated sound is not merely a sign that refers or implies this or that object, but rather it is a sign of a sign, or a form of a sign. This derivational development is particularly cogent in the case of homonyms, which in spite of their identical articulation generate different significations, as in for example, the Ukrainian *mylo* (soap) and *mylo* (kindly). Were the articulation of these two words their sole semantic marker, inevitably they would have produced semantic ambiguity. But inasmuch as the *mylo* in each derives from a different diachronic series, such ambiguity is virtually impossible for members of the same linguistic community.

The internal form of the word is the particular mode by which its intended content or reality is presented. Being polymorphic, these realities are usually rendered by only one of their attributes; hence words (or specifically, nouns) are metonymic representations or linguistic reductions of these realities.[10] For example, the word *stol* (table), which refers to an object with many attributes, is represented by a single one, that of "covering," present in its root *stl*. The word *okno* (window) refers to an object with such components as sills, glass, and so forth, but is represented solely by *oko* (eye), thus implying an object through which one looks. And the word *tuča* (cloud) is represented by the attribute of pouring, encoded in the root *tu* (to pour, to flow). Such representations (*predstavlenija*), Potebnja contended, are always ethnic (*narodnye*).[11] "The internal form of each of these

---

[9] Potebnja, *Iz zapisok po russkoj grammatike,* 1: 15.

[10] Humboldt illustrates the reductive nature of the internal form with the following examples: "In the German word *Vernunft* reposes the notion of taking (*das Nehmens*); in *Verstand* that of standing (*das Stehens*); and in *Blute* that of welling forth (*das Hervorquellens*)." *Linguistic Variability and Intellectual Development,* p. 71.

[11] Potebnja, *Iz zapisok po russkoj grammatike,* 1: 19.

words directs our thought differently,"[12] Potebnja concluded, because each language contains its own particular world view or a unique perspective.[13] Considered psychologically rather than linguistically, the internal form of the word is the focus of the "sensory image," that which is usually experienced in sense perception. But inasmuch as such an image contains a series of attributes that are in need of unity, only one of these attributes will normally dominate and generate the sense of a unified object. In this way, the dominant attribute functions within our consciousness as a partial representation or as a sign of the intended object. As such, it is the image of sensory images rather than the image of the object.[14]

The internal form of the word, due to its reductive function, greatly facilitates the cognitive process. Without it, in fact, this process would be considerably impeded. By reducing the polymorphic nature of intended realities to one of its attributes, the word becomes a communicable sign and can then be used in syntactic concatenations and in formations of symbols and concepts. The "sign within the word," Potebnja wrote, "is a necessary substitute for the corresponding image and concept (both for the acceleration of the thought and for the broadening of consciousness)."[15] In such communicative processes as speech, writing, and reading, many words lose the palpability of their

[12] Potebnja, "Mysl' i jazyk," p. 175.

[13] Humboldt discussed the relationship between language and the nation's spirit in his work *Agamemnon* and in "Über die Verschiedenheit des menschlichen Sprachbaues und ihren Einfluss auf die geistige Entwicklung des Menschengeschlechts." He wrote: "Language is as if the external appearance of the people's spirit; their language is their spirit and their spirit—their language. It is hardly possible not to think of them as identical" (p. 42). Humboldt, of course, was not alone in equating language with the spirit of the nation. German romantics and philosophers of the first half of the nineteenth century, notably Herder and Fichte, did the same: cf. J. G. Herder, *Sprachphilosophische Schriften* (Hamburg: F. Meiner, 1960), and J. G. Fichte, *Reden auf die deutsche Nation,* (Berlin: Deutsche Bibliothek, 1912). In the twentieth century, Humboldt's thesis that language forms the "intermediary world" between man and the external world, and thus encodes in its structure the particular ethnic *Weltanschauung,* has been embraced by a number of German linguists, philosophers, and psychologists. Notable among them are the philosopher Ernst Cassirer and the linguist Leo Weisgerber. In the United States this thesis has been adapted by Edward Sapir and Benjamin Whorf.

[14] Potebnja, "Mysl' i jazyk," p. 147.

[15] Potebnja, *Iz zapisok po russkoj grammatike,* 1: 17.

internal forms. "In most of them the connection with the previous ones is neither sensed by the speakers nor even known to scholarship."[16] Their signification "attaches itself directly to the sound, so that the connection between them seems to be arbitrary."[17] Hence it is to be assumed that their internal form is "completely empty (contentless) and that it acts as zero does in the Arabic notation of quanta; thus, the difference among 3.0, 30., and 0.3 depends upon the spot held by the zero."[18] However, internal forms in such words do not remain mute forever. They may be resuscitated either by our attention to their dormant images or by the syntactic context in which they occur.

Thus, while the external form and signification forever remain the inevitable conditions of the word's existence, the internal form, in most cases, tends to expire.

Already [Potebnja wrote] at the very origin of the word, there was inequity between its signification and representation (that is, the mode of this signification): *signification always contains more than does representation*. The word serves only as a fulcrum for the thought; but as the word is being applied to ever-new cases, this inequity grows correspondingly. The relatively broad and deep signification of the word ... tends to tear itself from the relatively insignificant representation ... but in this tendency it produces merely *a new word*. [Thus] the development of the language occurs through the dimming of representation.[19]

The internal form provides [us] "(a) with an awareness of the unity of complexes given in perception; (b) it establishes the unity of relations (of complexes) given only in their elements; (c) it *facilitates* generalization by removing what is immaterial (*idealization*) and thus increases the distance between human abstraction and the concrete-

---

[16] Ibid.

[17] Ibid.

[18] Ibid. Cf. also H. Steinthal, *Grammatik, Logik, und Psychologie: Ihre Prinzipien und ihr Verhältnis zu einander* (Berlin: F. Dümmler, 1855), p. 334.

[19] Potebnja, *Iz zapisok po teorii slovesnosti*, p. 21. Potebnja's definition of the functions of the internal form displays the influence of Kant's notion of transcendental schema, which is something like an empirical or sensible counterpart of the pure category—the fulcrum of which Potebnja spoke above.

ness of the living thoughts; (d) and it creates the category of thought objects."[20]

Finally, the third structural component of the word—the content, signification, or idea—subsists rather than exists in itself as an empirical given, since both external and internal forms of the word are more an indication (*ukazanie*) than a reproduction of it.[21] And yet both forms attain their identities interchangeably by bringing into our consciousness either this or that signification.

What and where is signification? Is it in language (speech) or in the creating and perceiving consciousness? It is in both, said Potebnja, for they coalesce: "The articulated sound pronounced by the speaker and perceived by the listener, stimulates in the latter a memory of his own similar sounds, which in turn invoke in his consciousness the thought of the object."[22] However, inasmuch as both participants of the speech act experience different sensory perception and apperceive the speech forms differently, the intended signification of the articulated sounds is necessarily at variance. While generating different objects, "the thoughts of both will have a common point of contiguity: representation (if it exists) and the formal signification of the word."[23]

"By signification one understands two distinct things, one of which (being the subject matter of linguistics) we shall call the immediate (*bližaščee*) and the other (the subject matter of other sciences) the extended (*dal'nejšee*) signification."[24] The internal form is a sign of the immediate signification. Being intersubjectively similar, this signification occurs in the consciousness of both the speaker and the listener, provided, of course, they both "belong to one and the same people."[25] As such, it is the formative organ of thought. Were it not for the continuous tendency for language to dim (*zatemnjat'*) its internal forms, and thereby to develop imageless words, people (as ethnic collectives) would remain forever locked in their particular perceptions of the world. Yet this dimming of internal forms does not

[20] Ibid., p. 20.
[21] Potebnja, *Iz zapisok po russkoj grammatike*, 1: 6.
[22] Potebnja, "Mysl' i jazyk," p. 139.
[23] Potebnja, *Iz zapisok po russkoj grammatike*, 1: 8.
[24] Ibid.
[25] Ibid., p. 9.

necessarily progress toward a total extinction of imaginative thoughts, because, as Potebnja put it, "the development of language occurs both as the *dimming* of representation and, due to new perception, the emergence of new imaginative words."[26]

The oblivion of the internal form or the "emptiness of the immediate signification"[27] reduces the word to pure form or sign of thought, rendering the external form the sole carrier of signification. Thus, the triune structure of the word becomes a dual one. In this case the signification may oscillate between personal/subjective and scientific/objective thoughts, depending upon the rigor of semantic conformity. "The difference in the degree of objectivity of thought is identical with the difference in the degree of its abstraction,"[28] that is, in the degree of the dimming of the word's internal form.

The extended signification of the word, unlike the immediate one, is semantically diffused; it cannot be brought to a common semantic denotation in speech. For both speaker and listener, even though their thought processes are anchored in one and the same utterance, this signification is at variance. Potebnja wrote, it "can be expressed by two triangles whose angles *b-a-c* and *d-a-e*, having a common apex *a* and being formed by the intersection of two lines, *be* and *cd*, are inevitably equal but everything else may be infinitely different."[29]

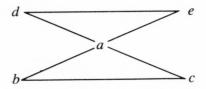

Apex *a* represents the immediate, and the two triangles *b-a-c* and *d-a-e* represent the extended significations. Each speech act therefore contains the immediate signification, the apex, and the extended signification, the triangles. From this one should infer that thinking only in images (in immediate significations) or only in imageless words (in extended significations) hardly exists in actuality. To put it

[26] Potebnja, "Mysl' i jazyk," p. 303.

[27] Potebnja, *Iz zapisok po russkoj grammatike*, 1: 8.

[28] Potebnja, "Mysl' i jazyk," p. 195.

[29] Ibid., p. 140.

differently, both thought and speech, cognitively and linguistically, are disproportionate quantities. Consequently, as Humboldt observed, "by the word no one thinks exactly the same thing as the other person does. . . . Each understanding is at the same time a non-understanding, each agreement in thoughts and feelings is likewise a disagreement."[30]

The distinction between the immediate and extended significations of the word is of key importance in Potebnja's literary theory, myth, and folklore. These "phenomena of language," studied either individually or collectively, attain their uniqueness through the two significations discussed above. In poetry, myth, and folklore, words with explicit representations dominate those without them, whereas in prose (science and scholarship), words with zero representation are the "only building material."[31] An exception to this paradigm is the intentional ambiguity in such literary constructs as satire, irony, anecdote, and fable, in which one internal form is intended to indicate two distinct significations simultaneously.[32]

All this seems to amend Potebnja's basic contention that poetry is thinking only in images and prose is thinking only in imageless words. By accepting as valid his definition and correlation for the two variables of signification, we cannot but infer that imaginative thinking does not and cannot exist without prosaic thinking, in the same way that an apex of a triangle cannot exist without the triangle itself.

Structural Constituents
of the Work of Poetic Art

Most of what has been said about the word, in and out of the syntactic setting, is applicable to the verbal arts. Potebnja observed: "In poetic, that is, artistic works in general, there are the same elements as in the word: *content* (or idea), which corresponds to the emotional image or the concept developed out of it; *internal form* [or image], which indicates the contents and corresponds to the representation (which has significance only as a symbol, an implication of a certain

---

[30] Humboldt, "Über die Verschiedenheit," p. 64.

[31] Potebnja, "Mysl' i jazyk," p. 195.

[32] Potebnja, *Iz zapisok po russkoj grammatike,* 4: 96.

aggregate of sense perception or of the idea); and finally, *external form,* in which the artistic image is objectified."[33]

The Word		The Work of Literary Art
external form (x)	↔	external form (x)
internal form (y)	↔	image (y)
signification (z)	↔	content/idea (z)

The three constituents of the work of poetic art are coextensive and interdependent. "The external form is indivisible from the internal one; it changes along with it, ceases to be itself, and yet it is, nevertheless, completely distinct from it."[34] The interdependence of x, y, and z implies that in an artistic configuration they have no value separately; that they are determined at once rather than sequentially; that such simultaneous determinations permit no radical variability in their configuration; that in case "consciousness loses the connection between the sound and significance, sound, aesthetically speaking, ceases to be the *external* form,"[35] becoming simply a mechanical disturbance in the air; and that each work of poetic art, in terms of its givens—x and y—is unique and can be rendered in no other way than its own, cannot be translated, paraphrased, or adapted because all such transpositions involve structural transformations.[36]

[33] Potebnja, "Mysl' i jazyk," p. 179.

[34] Ibid., p. 175.

[35] Ibid., p. 176.

[36] Potebnja, in spite of his indebtedness to Humboldt, did not share the latter's enthusiasm for translation. Humboldt believed that "translation, and especially that of the work of poets, is one of the most necessary undertakings in any literature, in part because it introduces certain forms of art and of humanity to those who are unfamiliar with the language and would, therefore, remain ignorant of them. Every nation is bound to gain a lot from doing this. But even more important, translation is to be done because it broadens the significance and the expressiveness of a given language." "Aeschylos *Agamemnon,*" in *Gesammelte Schriften,* 8: 130. Potebnja, on the other hand, believed that the poetic text is untranslatable, that "translation from one language into another is not a transmission of one and the same thought, but a stimulation of a distinctly different one." "Jazyk i narodnost'," p. 265.

The External Form

The external form of poetic art is that "verbal form which is significant in its constitutive parts."[37] How are we to understand this definition? By significant parts, Potebnja meant the selection and collocation of words that promote imaginative links among their euphony, their internal representation, and their intended content. The external form of poetic art, in order to be significant, must objectify in itself the artistic image, and thus be an indication of the intended thought or signification—"a hint at the certain totality of emotional percepts"[38]—otherwise it will be but a referent of an act of reference. Consequently, the "form of the work of poetic art is the word with the unity of sound and signification, rather than (merely) the sound, its primary external form."[39]

Psychologically, external form is the object of sensory perception, while internal form and signification are objects of cognition. To affect the synthesis of the aesthetic phenomena, however, the processes of perception and cognition are to be seen as complementary. Separately, they are either empty or sterile. Hence, those external forms which arouse only bewilderment, anger, fear, or excitement, and do not yield to semantic decoding, are aesthetically inferior to those forms which function as cognitive spectra. Aesthetically significant and valent forms, then, are inevitably bound up with cognition, or, as Kant would have it, the experience of the sensory impressions is possible only by the knowledge of the intellect. Therefore the structural concatenation of x and z by means of y, as a rule, precludes the aesthetic autonomy of any of these three constituents of the work of art. Such autonomy may occur only during the deliberate severance of x, y, and z. This severance may mean, insofar as the poet's creative act is concerned, a radical suspension of both an imaginative propensity of the poetic language and its semantic function, and, insofar as his *Lebenswelt* is concerned, an interruption of his affiliation with his linguistic and ethnic milieu. To Potebnja, the creation of poetic forms, when free from specific history and genesis, and detached from the subject, is a purposeless task. Does this mean that Potebnja's

---

[37] Potebnja, *Iz zapisok po teorii slovesnosti*, p. 30.

[38] Potebnja, "Mysl' i jazyk," p. 179.

[39] Ibid., p. 178.

theory cannot accommodate poetic avant-guardism, if by that one understands artistic forms that (due to their idiosyncratic character or overcoding in a given linguistic milieu) do not yield intersubjectively shared significations? External forms that are either "ahead of time" or "behind time" rather than "in time" are, in Potebnja's view, hardly aesthetically significant. "Everything," he wrote, "that narrows the realm of the observed phenomena renders the points of view one-sided, limits the means of expression, and leads to the downfall of the arts."[40] Even though works of poetic art are "created by minds that are superior to people,"[41] they are nevertheless intended for the aesthetic gratification of those people. "The weakness and absence of poetry," therefore, stands in direct proportion to the "alienation of the literary class from society, the restriction of the observed phenomena, the partiality of the point of view, and the paucity of the means of expression."[42]

In sum, the aesthetically significant external form is inseparable from the internal one. Jointly, as empirical givens, these forms excite our sense receptors, which in turn set into motion a complex apperceptive process. Our apprehension of the signification and the value of the intended phenomena and events issues out of this process. External forms, or sensory-motor patterns, are *terminus a quo* in this process. Without them no aesthetic experience can occur; yet it is the mode of these patterns that exerts a dominant influence upon the experience. Should they, for example, be interchangeable in every essential respect with those already existing in the perceiving mind and thus fuse unimpedingly with them, the apprehension of them will be either marginal or considerably retarded. Potebnja observed that "a series of objects, a', b', c', which are known to us and which present themselves to our perception gradually, will not be seen so long as they fuse unimpedingly with our previous percepts a, b, c. But if instead of the expected percept d, an unknown x, rather than a corresponding d', occurs; then the perception of the former, whose

---

[40] Potebnja, *Iz zapisok po teorii slovesnosti*, p. 117.
[41] Ibid.
[42] Ibid.

fusion with the previous one is being impeded, will be apperceived.''[43]

Aesthetic apprehension of external forms does not, however, result necessarily from a simple modal dichotomy between what is given and what is already known, as was asserted by the romantics and by the twentieth-century Russian formalists. The process of aesthetic apperception is far more complex than this. According to Potebnja, external forms that are aesthetically overcoded (or, in formalist terminology, are alienated) do not, as a rule, prompt the apperceptive process. If distributed on the imaginary axis $x \rightarrow y$ between radically overcoded and explicitly familiar forms, only those that invoke unity of disparate images in our consciousness will be apprehended as aesthetically significant. Such forms are not to be found on either pole of the axis, but rather somewhere at its center.

As objectively given components of poetic work, these external forms transform and perfect the corresponding aggregate in our mind and thereby function as a creating rather than a merely transmitting medium of significations—as *energeia* rather than *ergon*. To be aesthetically significant, they must be receptive to the semiotic approach.

The Internal Form

"Poetry," Potebnja stated, "is thinking in images ... without image there is no art, and especially, there is no poetry."[44] Image, internal form, representation, or symbolism—whatever one chooses to call the mode by which language seeks to evoke the sense of tangible realities—is of central importance to the poetic text.

While it was relatively simple to define the internal form of the word, inasmuch as Potebnja equated it with its etymon, the image of the work of poetic art eluded an easy definition.[45] His theory, in spite of the central importance of internal form, gave no definition of the

[43] Potebnja, "Mysl' i jazyk," p. 123.

[44] Potebnja, *Iz zapisok po teorii slovesnosti*, p. 83.

[45] For a historical survey of internal form, see Gustav Špet, *Vnutrennjaja forma slova (Ètjudy i variacii na temy Gumbol'ta)* (Moscow: Gosudarstvennaja Akademija xudožestvennyx nauk, 1927).

image. What follows, therefore, is an impartial elaboration of the image based on his theory as a whole.

Heeding Humboldt's axiom that "the most general aim of all arts is to transform reality into an image,"[46] Potebnja elevated the artistic image to hold the central category in his poetics. What is this category? The internal form of the word, to reiterate, is its closest etymological meaning, a relatively constant mode or a representative sign of the object. Within the work of poetic art, which is a syntactic fusion of *mots pleins,* the emerging image is either a progressively constructed collocation of such images (*sovokupnost' obrazov*) or a transcendent configuration of them. The two images are both theoretically and pragmatically dissimilar. The first resembles an algebraic group and depends upon the combinatory system of the given syntax, or, as Potebnja called it, upon the "modality of combination." Its elements, in varying degrees of completion, are distributed throughout the text. The second is a kind of nonadditive whole that is intentionally created at strategic points in the text or at the conclusion of it.

These two types of images can perform two distinct functions: the first aims to establish a similitude between the textual representation and the intended reality; and the second, to depict the "disproportion between representation and its signification."[47] In conventional terms, the first intends a realistic and the second a symbolic rendition of reality. In the first, "the poetic image . . . can be a faithful reproduction of reality; that is, its contents may not include anything that cannot be included in sober scientific thought or in ordinary daily perception."[48]

---

[46] Humboldt, "Über Goethes *Hermann und Dorothea,*" p. 126.

[47] Potebnja, *Iz zapisok po teorii slovesnosti,* p. 68.

[48] Ibid., p. 67. For example, such are the images in the following poem of A. A. Fet:

> Облаком волнистым
> Пыль встает в дали;
> Конный или пеший -
> Не видать в пыли.
> Вижу: кто то скачет
> На лихом коне.
> Друг мой, друг далекий,
> Вспомни обо мне!

> With a wavy cloud
> The dust rises in the distance;

In the second, on the other hand, "the poetic image, every time it is perceived and enlivened by the one who comprehends it, tells him something different and something more than what it directly contains."[49]

While recognizing the psychological and aesthetic possibilities of both processes, Potebnja favored the second as intellectually superior. He observed that "to those to whom poetic image is the focus of ten, twenty, thirty separate cases and to whom these cases have fused and formed an abstract conclusion, to those poetic image is more pithy and significant than to those to whom it says only what it contains."[50]

Primordially, the link between the image and signification was quasi-scientific or mythical: the image was directly transferable into signification. Their connection required neither validation nor verification—it was admissible on faith. The signifier and signified functioned as a semantic substitution or inversion. Once the two ceased to form an equation and became comparisons, however, their connection became poetic. Historically, this transition from myth to poetry began "with man's ability to realize and to retain the difference between the subjective beginning of the cognizing thought and that of its progression, which one can call (imprecisely) reality, world, or object."[51] Accordingly, in myth, the signifier and the signified can be expressed as $A \equiv X$ and in poetry as $A = X$.

Images of both types (cf. p. 43) are the linguistic means, or as Potebnja put it, the leap from representation to signification. So long as they remain "constant predicates to [their] changing subjects [or] a constant explanation of the changing *explenandum*,"[52] they remain aesthetically significant. Should they figure as equivalences of the

---

Is it a rider or a pedestrian?
One cannot see in the dust.
I see someone is galloping
On a dashing horse.
My friend, my faraway friend,
Remember me!

[49] Ibid., p. 69. In Potebnja's view, Heine's poem "Ein Fichtenbaum steht einsam," and Lermontov's and Tjutčev's translations of it, illustrate the disproportion between representation and signification.

[50] Potebnja, *Iz lekcij po teorii slovesnosti*, p. 521.

[51] Potebnja, *Iz zapisok po teorii slovesnosti*, p. 590.

[52] Ibid., p. 484.

intended realities, however, as they did in myth, the images automatically assume a didactic role.

Poetry (that is, the creative arts and myth) and prose (that is, science) are not completely unrelated. While structurally they are indeed different, functionally they are merely two modes of cognition. "Both go from reality ... toward something that does not belong to it." Consequently, "reality and idea are common constituents of poetry and prose; in both of them [our] thought strives to introduce connection and completion into the diversity of sensory data; but the different means and results peculiar to them demand that these two quests of [our] thought support and complement each other so long as mankind is 'striving.' "[53] As to their means and results, Potebnja observed:

> The common formula of poetry (respective art) is A (image) $< X$ (significance); that is, between image and signification there always exists an inequality such that A is less than X. The establishment of equality between A and X would destroy the poeticalness, would convert the image into a prosaic designation of a particular case, deprive it of the relationship with something else, or would even convert it into a scientific fact and its signification into a rule. X in relation to A is always something different, often even heterogeneous. Poetic thinking is an explanation of a particular by another heterogeneous particular. Thus if prose is *allegoria,* in a broad sense of this word, then both prose, as an expression of elementary observation and science, tend in some sense to become *tautologia.*[54]

In brief, the internal form of the work of poetic art is a linguistic component of the text, and as such should not be confounded with "another representation that is more known than defined, and that is the same as perception, emotional image, or an aggregate of attributes."[55] By distinguishing the two—one as a linguistic *given* and

---

[53] Potebnja, "Mysl' i jazyk," p. 193.

[54] Potebnja, *Iz zapisok po teorii slovesnosti,* p. 100.

[55] Potebnja, *Iz zapisok po russkoj grammatike,* 1:7. Steinthal, whose psycholinguistic model Potebnja emulated closely, defined internal form more psychologically than linguistically: "The internal form of language is to be regarded as the cause, as the stimulus that generates the sound; it is, however, an unconscious, instinctive, and mechanically operating cause that in and of itself does not aim at associating with or building the language sound out of the tone it arouses. Upon generating it,

another as a psychological experience—Potebnja takes a stand apart from those psychologistic positions which conceive of poetic images solely as experiences of either the external or the intraorganic realities determined by the idiosyncratic complexities of individual perceivers.

The poetic text—due to its internal forms, or, as phenomenological theory would have it, due to its aspects (*Anschauungen*)—affects our perception and cognition, and thus renders the intersubjective knowledge of it a continuous possibility. A constancy of the internal form does not, however, guarantee its permanence. In time it may, as it often does, lose its palpability, and thus cease to elicit aesthetic responses and to generate corresponding significations. In this way the poetic text becomes a mere historical artifact.

The Content

"By the content of the picture or the novel," Potebnja wrote, "we understand a series of thoughts that are either aroused by images in the onlooker or the reader or that served as a basis of the image in the creator himself at the time of his creative act."[56] From this definition, we can infer that the work of poetic art, as an autonomously existing artistic given, consists of two rather than three constituents: the external and internal forms. The third component—content or idea—exists only as a semantic potentiality. In order for it to emerge during aesthetic heteronomy, the work must possess the "strength of its internal forms," and the perceiver's mind (*duša*) must in turn be in need of structural coalescence. The content of the work of poetic art is therefore the result of a dyadic relationship. Unlike the external and internal forms that exist objectively, the content subsists in the perceiving consciousness of the creator and his audience. Potebnja observed:

During the creation of the poetic work, at the moment when *X* is being explained by means of *A, a* occurs. However, in comprehension, the listener or the reader is provided first of all with a sign *a*, which must be explained with the reserve of [his] previous thought, *A*. To [him] *a*

---

another property of the soul transforms the blindly begotten tone into an intentional sound." *Grammatik, Logik und Psychologie,* p. 343.

[56] Potebnja, "Mysl' i jazyk," p. 176.

ought to serve as an indication of x which is being cognized by [him]. The analogy between creative and cognitive acts indicates that we can comprehend poetic work to the extent that we participate in its creation.[57]

Potebnja's position on the content of poetic work poses some difficult questions. If the work of poetic art "consists only of symbols of the extra linguistic signification and, in regard to the latter, is only the form,"[58] then at what point in the "modality of combination" of these symbols does its content emerge—throughout its unfolding, from its beginning to its end, or only at certain points? Is the final content a "collocation of images"[59] of "close significations" of each sentence of the text, or is it the signification of significations, the content that transcends the sum total of its parts? Is the perceiver's content a variable of the content intended by the author and thus dependent upon it, or is it a distinct constituent of the mental processes that emerge as a cognitive response in each interpreter and thus independent of it?

Potebnja's theory does not provide explicit answers to these and similar questions. Implicitly, however, the statement "a complex artistic work is exactly the same kind of development of the main image as the complex sentence is the development of one emotional image"[60] infers the following arguments.

In the process of perception, the final content of the work of poetic art results from the changes in structure and form that occur during the transition of individual images from their emergence to their conclusion. Individual images, in order to yield content, are to be arranged in some relation of subordination and interdependence. The main image is either a complex that consists of subordinates or an idea of the intended object, graspable in the sensibly perceptible form.

As to the process that leads to the emergence of such an idea, Potebnja, almost anticipating the structural linguists, believed that the content of the work is formed sequentially. During each instant of perception, our consciousness holds only one of the text's semantic

---

[57] Potebnja, *Iz lekcij po teorii slovesnosti*, p. 543.

[58] Potebnja, *Iz zapisok po russkoj grammatike*, 1:65.

[59] Potebnja, *Iz lekcij po teorii slovesnosti*, p. 549.

[60] Potebnja, "Mysl' i jazyk," p. 188.

units and extracts the signification available to it at that instant. Upon the completion of the perceptive act, it readjusts the accumulated significance to the central one. "At the moment when we are pronouncing the last word of the sentence, we think directly only of the content of this word; however, this content indicates what it refers to and what it has derived from, first [it indicates] other words of the same sentence that preceded it, then [it indicates] the sense of the sentence, chapter, book."[61] Semantic units that preceded in focus, Potebnja believed, retreat "beyond the limits of the threshold"[62] and from out there, "some representations exhibit more pronounced influence upon the cognized [phenomenon], some less. Those which are unrelated to the thought occupying us at that moment cannot occur in the subsequent one, provided external impressions do not interrupt the flow of our thought and do not give it a new direction. Each member of the cognized series of representations brings into consciousness the results of all the preceding ones. The more versatile the connections among the preceding members, the more significant are these results for us."[63] As Jan Mukařovský put it,[64] the perception of the poetic text occurs on both horizontal and vertical axes simultaneously: the first is structured by the text and the second by our apperception of it. From the interaction of these two processes results the transformation of the perception of the poetic text into a cognition of it. According to Potebnja:

A new perception, while fusing with the preceding one, inevitably brings it into consciousness or at least creates an incomprehensible situation for us that we shall call movement; but due to the fact that the preceding perception was posited either together or in some connection with other [perceptions], they, too, enter [our] consciousness. Thus through such fusion a link occurs between those representations which in time and in sequence of their appearance in [our] mind [soul] were, originally, not linked together. Along with this device that arouses in [our] consciousness some previous representations, there is also a device that removes others; if, for example, a new perception *C* has most

---

61 Ibid., p. 175.
62 Ibid., p. 142.
63 Ibid., p. 135.
64 Cf. Jan Mukařovský, *The Word and Verbal Art: Selected Essays,* trans. John Burbank and Peter Steiner (New Haven and London: Yale University Press, 1977).

of the common points with one of the previous perceptions A rather than with B, which is in [our] consciousness, then B will be pushed out from the thought by A's attraction to it. A and B are thus linked, the first with D, E, F, the second with G, H, I, and [therefore] can be regarded as the beginning of a series that through them enters consciousness; the thought, following the direction whose beginning is A, removes another direction B, but the identity of C with A and not with B is forever a definable and invariable quantity: it is changeable in the same way as the feeling that accompanies and changes the coloring of perception and, in turn, depends upon the imperceptible alterations in the content of the latter.[65]

From this rather opaque description it is evident that the content of the poetic work, as it appears in our consciousness, is not an indiscriminate computation of all of the work's semantic components, but instead an intentional correlation of what is being selected, retained, transformed, and, of course, amplified by our apperception. To borrow the Gestalt term, the potential content of the poetic work and its realization in our consciousness are seldom, if ever, isomorphic.

The disclosure of the content of the work of poetic art, in addition to being structured by its text and by the reader's apperception, is also affected by the historical context in which it is intended and in which it is generated. Inasmuch as neither the poet nor the perceiver can transcend his historicity, the disclosed content stands to be intersubjectively similar. Theoretically, while the content of the poetic work might indeed be a hardly known quantity (*mnimoizvestnaja veličina*), historically, the content that we think, by belonging also to others, is bound to be similar.

Conclusion

The structure of the work of poetic art, being analogous to the word, consists of three fundamental components: external form, image, and content. The first two, as linguistic givens, constitute its constant artistic components; the third, its variable semantic potential-

---

[65] Potebnja, "Mysl' i jazyk," p. 136.

ity. All three exist in a peculiar synchronic simultaneity, so that the suspension of one inevitably results in the suspension of all. Nevertheless, from the emblematic and the functional points of view, the image is the central component of the work's structure.

Poetic image, if constructed step by step, is a combination of selectively related representations contained in the *mots pleins* and—if created at strategic points of the text—an internal form of a lexeme whose vividness dominates other forms in a given syntactic surrounding. Historically, the former has been favored by narrative and the latter by lyrical texts. The aesthetic value of the poetic image is contingent upon the attribute of the intended objects that subsumes and evokes their totality. All poetic images, therefore, regardless of whether they are verbal substitutions or contiguities, are metonymic.

Insofar as all languages are embedded in ethnic consciousness, poetic images reflect, *ipso facto,* the congenial structure of the world. Confronting poetic imagery, outer and inner, the human mind either equates or correlates it with intended realities and conceives of it either as myth or as distinct phenomena and thus as poetry. Images of the former are posited as equivalences and those of the latter as *tertium comparationis* or, in linguistic terms, as predicates with potentially multiple subjects. In reality, however, these two modes of perception are seldom clearly demarcated: in myth there are resorts to poetics, and in poetry to prosaic imagery.

The content of the work of poetic art, insofar as it is represented attributively rather than totally, is incessantly in *statu nascendi.* A genuine work of poetic art generates multiple contents; however, within a linguistically congenial milieu, the generative power of images is contained by the commonly shared, relatively stable, and objectively given representations of reality contained in them. Therefore, the creation, perception, and cognition of poetic images occurs within the limiting context of the collective vision of the world.

The content (if by this we understand, as Potebnja did, "an answer to a certain x")[66] is realized either progressively from the beginning to the end of the temporal unfolding of the work, or abruptly at specific points of the text. In the first instance, the content is the integral of the significations of all the preceding images; in the second, it is the

---

[66] Potebnja, *Iz lekcij po teorii slovesnosti,* p. 549.

differential of a "series of thoughts evoked by images,"[67] distributed throughout the text.

From the perspective of the current discussion of linguistic and literary structures, Potebnja's view might appear rather inchoate. In the context of the sensationalist psychology prevalent in his time, which insisted on what Cassirer called the "dogma of autarchy and autonomy, the self-sufficiency and self-evidence of perceptual knowledge,"[68] the view was audacious. In fact, Potebnja, far in advance of transformational structuralism, postulated the system of psycholinguistic transformation whereby cognitive constructions are determined by linguistic structures.

In contrast to today's structuralists, who tend to eliminate the epistemic subject, Potebnja perceived it to be the very center of all mental operations. Even though this subject per se cannot be fully determined because "after becoming the object of (our) observation it changes substantially and ceases to be itself,"[69] it is nevertheless an "internal eye" that, while unable to see itself, alternately either focuses on the stage of our mental experiences or averts itself from it. Hence the content of our consciousness—the cognized I (*soznavaemoe ja*), the empirical I that we know—cannot occur without the activity of the cognizing I (*soznajuščee ja*), the pure I that escapes definition. This being the case, it was plausible for Potebnja to posit that the relationship between the former and the latter, at least in their developed form, as consciousness and self-consciousness, occurs through language. Thus, the "whatness" of the objective reality, while being transposed into the apperceptive mass of our consciousness, becomes pure linguisticity, and as such is subjected to the determination of the language structure.

What then is the genesis of structure in a work of poetic art? Does such work contain it simply because it is a linguistic construct? Or is it structure created during the dyadic intercourse between the poetic text and its aesthetic apperception? Potebnja definitely favored a third position. The triune structure of the work of poetic art, consisting of the external and internal forms and the content, emerges in the course of aesthetic apperception. Prior to the act of reading, the work awaits

---

[67] Potebnja, "Mysl' i jazyk," p. 176.
[68] Cassirer, *Philosophy of Symbolic Forms,* 3: 205.
[69] Potebnja, "Mysl' i jazyk," p. 169.

its completion through apperception. Structure, in Potebnja's definition, is, therefore, a contingent creation. In order for it to emerge, the poetic text, consisting of two structural givens, must be actualized by the language of the epistemic subject.

CHAPTER THREE

The Modality of Poetic Forms

Immanent Forms

Potebnja discerned two kinds of forms: those that constitute the very essence of poetic language and are independent of man's varying creative intentionality, and those that result precisely from such an intentionality. Consequently, verbal constructs, be they myth, folklore, poetry, or prose, can be looked upon as configurations of both immanent and intentional forms, and their classification can be attempted on the basis of both. Seen from the former, the distinction between these constructs is determined by the semantic function of their internal form. So long as, for example, the proverb, one of the most concise poetic constructs, continues to explain varied existential events, it remains a poetic allegory. When, however, its internal form begins to refer to only one specific event, it automatically converts into a prosaic statement. Hence, the proverb, in terms of its immanence, has only two semantic manifestations. On the other hand, a protean and complex verbal construct such as the novel, in addition to its capacity for polysemy, can also perform distinctly referential or prosaic functions. It follows that pure poetry and pure prose are but terminal thresholds on a hypothetical axis between which language distributes fluxional ratios of imaginative and conceptual syntactics. Mathematics represents a language on the extreme right of such an axis.

Historically, the progression from poetry to prose was preceded by grammatically unstructured words. Pre-poetic perception, Potebnja alleged, did not distinguish among the object, its qualities, and its instrumentality. Such discernment must have been a matter of continuous linguistic evolution. Hence such grammatical categories as verb, noun, and adjective have developed and continue to do so in the sentence.[1] The etymology of adjectives and nouns reveals their common source; for example, Russian *goluboj* (blue) from the color of a *golub* (dove) and *solovoj* (yellow) from *solovej* (nightingale); Polish *niebieski* (light blue) from *niebo* (sky); and so forth.

Originally, Potebnja asserts, sentences must have been the comparison of two substantives or two independently formed emotional images. In all probability they were initially cognitive attempts to divide images of corresponding objects into their constituent attributes, then to compare them, and eventually to form a rudimentary analytical judgment. This must have been the beginning of man's attempt to conceive reality linguistically.

The progression from the inchoate pre-poetic construct to conceptual prose, however, must not be considered as irreversibly unilinear, because such a progression would necessarily lead to the eventual disappearance of imaginative thought and the total triumph of conceptual thinking. "Differentiation of poetry and prose," Potebnja wrote, "does not lead to the death of poetry,"[2] inasmuch as the imaginative character might disappear in individual words but not in the language as a whole. Its congruent character, simultaneously poetic and prosaic, evolves from the creation of new words as well as from an ever-new combination of the existing ones, thus protracting its multifunctionality.

What, then, are folklore, poetry, and prose from the perspective of their immanent forms? All three are narrative sequences, articulated in accordance with preexistent grammatical rules; all have either a dynamic or an inert internal form; and all are directed toward some implicit or explicit goal. The internal form of the first and second, "in relation to its variable content, remains immobile,"[3] whereas that of the third is inert. Its intended reference is contained by its external form. The difference between folklore and poetry, on the other hand, is due to the fact that the former has existed in oral and the latter in written versions, and, correspondingly, in textual variability and relative permanence. Authentic folk song, for example, "during its life span is not just one work, but a series of variants whose ends can be greatly dissimilar but whose intermediary levels fuse imperceptibly

---

[1] Potebnja, "Mysl' i jazyk," p. 151.
[2] Potebnja, *Iz zapisok po teorii slovesnosti*, p. 103.
[3] Ibid., p. 139.

with one another.''[4] Writing, by contrast, has generally fostered conscious and unintentional conservation; through assimilation, contraction, abbreviation, and omission, it has often led to the formation of its own language. Oral or colloquial language, however, has always favored communally shared forms of reference, devices, and representation. Oral poetry resorts to fixed measure, melody, and mannered expression. Folk poets seldom consider their works as exclusively their own. The creation and the perception of such poetry are practically identical acts; deviation from the existing patterns occurring in a collectively shared inventory of devices is dilatory and insignificant, even though each repetition is always somewhat different in rendition and content. As with poetry in general, folk poetry is not "work (*ergon*) but activity (*energeia*), not song but *nomen actionis,* singing.''[5]

The specific modality of oral poetry emanates from the relationship of its symbols to the intended reality or reference. There are three such relationships: first, either explicit correspondence or explicit difference between symbol and reference; second, contraposition between symbol and reference; and third, causal relationship between symbol and reference.

The first, usually rendered as distich (positive or negative correspondence between two objects) is symmetrical, as for example, in this Ukrainian song:

> Грушиця моя! чом ти не зелена?
> "My pear tree! Why aren't you green?"

> Милая моя! чом ти не весела?
> "My darling! Why aren't you happy?"

Grammatically, such correspondences may be juxtaposed as apposition (pear tree/darling); as an adverbial modifier in the instrumental case (in Russian: *solncem blestet'*, 'to shine like a sun'), or as a developed sentence in which the intended reference is implied contextually (in Czech: "Ach ty róže, krasná rože! Čomu si rano rozkevětla, rozkvětavši pomrzla, pomrzavši usvědla, usvědevši opadla?"

---

[4] Ibid., p. 143.
[5] Ibid.

"Rose, beautiful rose! Why did you blossom so early, after blossoming freeze, after freezing fade, after fading fall off?"). A negative comparison may be constructed as a "not/but" opposition or as a question and answer (in Serbian):

> Šta se sjaji kroz goru zelenu?
> Da l'je sunce, da l'je jasan mesec?
> Nit'je sunce, ni ti jasan mesec,
> Već zet šuri na vojvodstvo dođe.

> What's glittering through the green forest?
> Is it the sun or the bright moon?
> Neither the sun nor yon bright moon,
> But the son-in-law coming to the brother-in-law's
>   dukedom [to pay homage].

In contraposition, the form is similar to that of the extended sentence, as for example, in a Ukrainian song where carefree birds are contraposed with the figure of a worrisome and aging woman.

> Над горою високою голуби літають.
> Я розкоші не зазнала, а літа минають.

> Over the high mountain doves are flying:
> I have experienced no luxury, yet the years are passing.

In a causal relationship, two objects are linked symbolically on account of their alleged similarities. Such linkage is used in various medicinal charms, symbolic cures, and superstitions; for example, "If your ears ring, somebody is speaking about you." As a portent (*primeta*) this expression must have been coined due to some associative or congruent points, such as sound, distinctive marks, and action; however, portents, as verbal constructs inferring a causal relationship between disparate objects, are seldom empirically true. As abundantly attested to by colloquial language, these linkages must have been made on the basis of an external similarity rather than a uniform coexistence and sequence. For example, "it would be impossible to explain," Potebnja wrote, "how man began curing the disease erysipelas and others by fire if one loses sight of the fact that prior to this there must have existed an association between fire and disease, a representation of the latter by fire."[6] "More than likely," he continued, "man originally became aware of the cause through creating it by sorcery or similar phenomena"[7] based on language.

These forms of folklore are more than mere devices with which nameless bards composed songs, fairy tales, superstitions, mythical stories, proverbs, *dumas, bylinas*, and so on. Indeed, they were the very mode of man's understanding of the unity and disparity of his world. One example is a modern Ukrainian folk song:

> І по той бік гора
> І по сей бік гора.
> А між тими та гіроньками
> Ясная зоря;
> О, тож не ясна,
> О, тож, тож моя та дівчинонька
> По воду пішла.

> And on that side there is a mountain.
> And on this side there is a mountain.
> And between these two mountains
> There is a bright star;
> Oh, it isn't a bright [star],
> Oh, it is my girlfriend
> Who went to fetch water.

This song might appear to be merely a simple negative simile; yet, from a historical and conceptual perspective, its juxtaposition of positive and negative oppositions must have been a model of explicatory reasoning. Potebnja observed: "The first scientific explanation of the fact corresponds to positive comparison; the theory that annihilates this explanation corresponds to simple negation. To man, in whose eyes comparisons contained in language were science (*nauka*) and wisdom, poetic negation was already a type of destructive criticism."[8]

In individually created poetic art, and by this Potebnja meant belles lettres in general, the relationships between symbol and reference evolved into a complex system of tropes, notably metaphor and

---

[6] Potebnja, "Mysl' i jazyk," p. 204.
[7] Ibid.
[8] Ibid., p. 208.

metonymy.[9] In such poetry, unlike in folklore where it was determined by the genetic affinities, comparison, and contra-position have frequently been affected by various intellectual considerations.

Poetic tropes, Potebnja observed, are not synonymous with poetic images or internal forms. They are the "mode of transition" or the "leap" from images to signification,[10] and can be of two kinds— "images believed to be objective and thereby transferable into signification as they are, and images as a subjective means toward signification."[11] The first mode figures prominently in mythical, and the second in poetic perceptions.

Metaphor, or, more generally, "metaphoricity," is that quality of language whereby "any subsequent signification (*respective* word) may be created only by means of the preceding one that is distinct from it. As a result, it is possible to create an infinite quantity of derivatives from a finite number of relatively elementary words."[12] In this sense, "metaphoricity is a perennial quality of language,"[13] and the significations it generates are but a transition from metaphor to metaphor. And yet, Potebnja observed, to treat language as nothing but metaphor, or, as Derrida says, as pure figuration, would prevent us from knowing anything at all. While we may indeed never be able to reach demonstrative truth (because concepts that allegedly represent it can never become final), the distinction between metaphor and signification assures the possibility of science and of effective communication.

In a limited sense, metaphor "is a transfer of a word that is unrelated . . . to the signification that is being sought, either from type to appearance, or from appearance to type, or from appearance to appear-

---

[9] Hyperbole and irony, generally considered as separate tropes, are not, in Potebnja's view, distinct, because they do not represent a specific relation of the image and its signification.

[10] Potebnja, *Iz zapisok po teorii slovesnosti,* p. 407. Potebnja was well acquainted with the vast literature on poetic tropes. His definitions are frequently definitions *per contra.* His lecture notes are replete with quotations from Aristotle, Quintillian, Wackernagel, Paul, Benfey, Taine, Spencer, etc.

[11] Ibid., p. 406.

[12] Ibid., p. 589.

[13] Ibid.

ance, or by correspondence (similarity)."[14] Metaphor by correspondence is not merely a substitution of two known quantities (as, for example, Aristotelian poetics claimed), but an authentic attempt to define the unknown in terms of the known. Aristotle's equation $a:b = c:d$, Potebnja said, implies a "senseless game of replacement of the existing quantities rather than a serious search for truth."[15] In order to be a true metaphor this correspondence must include a signification that is being sought; it must be $a:b = c:x$. Otherwise, metaphor would be but a stale catachresis. Potebnja added: "Aristotle's speculation about the mutual substitution of two members in the metaphoric proportion would be valid if language and poetry did not contain a definite direction of cognition from the previously cognized to the unknown, or if the conclusion of analogy in metaphor was merely an aimless game in the transfer of the ready, given quantities instead of a serious search for the truth."[16]

In metonymic constructions that include synedoche, the image represents reference by one of its attributes or, conversely, the attributes by their reference (*pars pro toto* or *totum pro parte*). Thus they either amplify or reduce the intended reference. Unlike metaphor, which relates phenomena of different order (as, for example, nature and human life), metonymy relates phenomena that stand in an objective relationship to one another. In a strictly linguistic sense, most communicative signs are metonymic.

In some instances these two major tropes cannot be readily distinguished. For example, the expression "burning heart" may be regarded as either metaphor or metonymy, depending upon whether we consider "burning" a substantive, that is, an independent phenomenon, or an attribute implicit in the notion of heart. As "leaps from the image to signification," tropes may take two different values—mythic and poetic—given the attitude our consciousness takes toward them. In other words, they are one or the other only in regard to the thought of those by whom and for whom they were created. In poetic works they function as the means of creating or of making us aware of signification. As such, they decompose into their elements or are destroyed every time they reach their object. In this

[14] Ibid., p. 261.
[15] Ibid.
[16] Ibid.

sense they serve only an allegorical purpose. In myth, on the other hand, they function differently. By not being realized by the subject, they are completely transferred into signification without decomposing. Myth "is, therefore, a verbal expression of an explanation (apperception) in which the explaining image, which has only the subjective meaning, is imbued with objectivity and true being in the explained."[17] In other words, it is a statement whose signifier and signified, in spite of their explicit semantic variance, are perceived as complementary.

Even though prevalent in folkore or collective art, myth is by no means absent in individually created works. In Potebnja's view, it is a fundamental human disposition affecting all possible significations— religious, philosophical, and scientific.

Generally speaking, myth "belongs to the sphere of poetry and, like any poetic work, is an answer to a certain question of [our] thought and thus a quantitative augmentation of previous cognition; it consists of image and signification whose unity need not be verified, as is the case in science, and can still be directly convincing, that is, accepted on faith; and as a result, it is seen as a product that terminates the act of cognition and that differs [from this act] by being unconscious. Myth, initially, is a verbal work that always precedes the pictorial or plastic depiction of mythical image."[18]

Potebnja's definition of myth and poetic tropes implies the essential identity of the human mind in history.[19] Accordingly, it perseveres

---

[17] Ibid., p. 587.

[18] Ibid., p. 586.

[19] This definition sets Potebnja apart from a group of scholars contemporary to him: Max F. Müller (1823–1900), Aleksandr N. Afanas'ev, and even Aleksandr N. Veselovskij (1838–1906) who treated myth diachronically. Müller's theory of myth (cf. his *Comparative Mythology* [New York: Arno Press, 1977], and *Lectures on the Science of Language* [New York: C. Scribner, 1865]), based on the assumption that myth was the "disease of language," was particularly objectional to Potebnja. In his view this assumption implied that prior to myth, language must have been superior in its generalizing and communicative functions. "Such exultation of thought, and its subsequent degradation are unjustifiable and contradict the theory of the gradual evolution of thought. They contradict M. Müller's assertion itself about the original concreteness of language." *Iz zapisok po teorii slovesnosti,* p. 423. Müller's assumption also implied a stage in the evolution of language when it was not metaphorical. This, Potebnja insisted, was wrong, since "metaphoricity was the only original way acces-

without essential change. Even "the most positive contemporary mind that occupies itself with chemical analyses, comparative anatomy, statistical conclusions, and the like would name and consider the cloud to be a cow if it had only as much knowledge about the cloud and the cow as the ancient Aryan had." Hence, if "images that are identified in language and myth seem to us to be very much different, then it is only due to the peculiarity of our point of view."[20] The identity and comparison of objects, in myth and poetry respectively, is a matter of noetic faculty rather than a functional decay of language. "With the insufficiency of observation, with the extremely weak awareness of this insufficiency, and with the intentional attempt to compensate for it, the identity of these images must have appeared so great that it could have been only a matter of a sane mind rather than of stupidity."[21]

Finally, the difference between myth and poetic art lies in the fact that the former relates to only one referent while the latter is a predicate to an unrestricted number of referents. Therefore, "that cloud which was called a mountain, or that sun which was presented as a wheel of light, were completely different from the cloud represented by a cow or the sun represented as a 'fire-bird' (*žar-ptica*)."[22] Even when man became capable of abstracting different objects as one and the same, instead of subsuming their multiple representations by one lexical code, he conceived of them as transformational sequences; instead of saying, "it only seems to me that the sun is a bird, but actually it is the wheel of a chariot," he said, "the being that governs the solar chariot occasionally becomes a bird." Such mythical transformations, Potebnja contended, abound in fairy tales and superstitions.

The singularity of referent in myth, from the point of view of its function, renders it equipollent to science. "Myth," Potebnja stated, "is similar to science in that it aims at objective knowledge of the world,"[23] or that, like science, "it is an act of conscious thought, an act of cognition, an explanation of *X* by the aggregate of the

---

sible to language. [Generalizing power] presupposes the absence of representation in the word and its prosaic character." (Ibid., p. 591).

[20] Ibid., p. 593.

[21] Ibid.

[22] Ibid.

[23] Potebnja, "Mysl' i jazyk," p. 171.

previously given attributes, united and brought to consciousness by the word or by the image of A."[24] From the perspective of its composition, myth, however, is closer to poetry than to science. In myth, as in poetry, the image is manifestly present, whereas in science it is absent. Algorithmically, the three can be shown) this way:

$$\text{myth:} \quad X \equiv a \, (A)$$

$$\text{poetry:} \quad X = a < A$$

$$\text{science:} \quad X \equiv A$$

in which X stands for signification, reference, or the cognized object; a for image, attribute, or metonymic representation of X; and A for the aggregate of the previously acquired knowledge pertinent to X.

Intentional Forms

Unlike immanent forms that originate in linguistic and ethno-psychological structures, the intentional forms of the work of poetic art are a matter of the poet's creative choice—his aesthetic judgment and preference determine its generic appearance. The poet has no such conscious choice with internal forms, for although he might enhance or blur their expressiveness, he cannot avoid them. In poetic art, external and internal forms are, to use Kant's terminology, a priori and necessary.[25]

This, of course, does not mean that artistic genres can be suspended altogether. It merely means that they are subject to the continuous vicissitudes of aesthetic predilection. The aesthetic necessity of

[24] Potebnja, *Iz zapisok po teorii slovesnosti*, p. 401.

[25] Potebnja shared a number of Kant's aesthetic assumptions, but in regard to intentional forms, he seemed to profess a somewhat different position than Kant's. Kant believed that aesthetic intention was also preexistent and necessary. The very fact that the artist imbues this or that experience with specific forms is proof that they are necessary. To make sense of his experience the poet has no alternative but to determine its formal purposiveness. His aesthetic judgment, therefore, contains a principle of a priori. Cf. Kant's *The Critique of Judgment*, especially the first part, "Critique of Aesthetic Judgment."

immanent forms and the temporal relativity of intentional ones, there-fore, render the former primary and the latter secondary in the classification of poetic texts. "We can see poetry," Potebnja wrote, "in any verbal work in which the definition of the image, by a few of its features, generates fluctuation of signification—a *mood*—and by which it sees in them a great deal more than they contain, and in which—without, or even contrary to, the author's intention—allegory appears."[26] No matter whether it is a simple poetic statement or a "universally recognized novel or novella, poetry is everywhere where it is most concentrated, potent, and pure."[27] Combined with prose, it might also be in scientific or journalistic literature.

Traditionally, poetic texts, when seen from the perspective of inten-tional forms, have been classified as epic, lyric, or dramatic. Depend-ing upon the authority of the existing convention, Potebnja alleged that these categories may or may not facilitate the imaginative rendi-tion of the intended reality. If they do, they enhance the heuristic power of the poetic text; otherwise, they are merely decoration. Also, if they do, then they relate to the intended referent in the same way that the "form of the crystal, plant, and animal does to the processes that have generated it":[28] if they do not, then they are "completely separable from such a content."[29]

Potebnja's definition of the three generic groups was very close to that of the German romantics, particularly Goethe and Schiller.[30] Thus epic poetry, both simple (historical and autobiographical) and com-plex (novella, novel, short story), as *perfectum* is a "calm reflection, objectivity (an absence of any other personal interest in things de-picted, except the one that is needed for the possibility of the

---

[26] Potebnja, *Iz zapisok po teorii slovesnosti*, p. 108.

[27] Ibid., p. 107.

[28] Ibid., p. 108.

[29] Ibid.

[30] In the famous document "Über epische und dramatische Dichtung," Goethe and Schiller defined the difference between epic and drama thus: "An epic poet narrates an event as completely past, while the dramatic poet presents it as completely present. . . . The rhapsodist as a higher being ought not to appear in the poem himself; at best he should stay behind a curtain, so that we can separate everything personal from his work and can believe we are hearing only the voice of the Muses in general." Johann W. Goethe, *Sämtliche Werke*, 40 vols. (Stuttgart und Berlin: T. G. Cotta, 1902–1907), 36: 149.

depiction itself.)"[31] Its manner of narration is free from "haphazard leaps, interruption, and gaps."[32] Unlike the lyrical mode, which prefers metaphors, it relies greatly upon metonymy. It "expands the time limits in the form of digressions (retrospective narration)."[33] In its simple form it removes the narrator from the center of action and keeps him hidden—he is "not seen." Events or series of events are related causally. Cause "may appear either as external powers or as internal properties of phenomena. As the former it may appear as miraculous in the mythological sense; as the latter, as miraculous in the scientific sense. But no matter what we call this chain of causes and effects—God, fate, or the world—it nonetheless remains irrational and inaccessible to our comprehension."[34]

Lyric poetry, in all of its variety—erotic, contemplative, elegiac, sonnet—is *praesens*. As such, it "speaks about future and past only to the extent that the 'objective object' disturbs, worries, attracts, or repulses us. Hence the properties of lyrical representation are brevity, reticence, and so-called lyrical disorder."[35] As a cognition, "it objectivizes emotion, subordinates it to thought, calms it down, moves it into the past, and thus enables us to master it."[36] This direct tie with existential involvements renders the lyrical poem more pragmatic than the epic. As a variant of $X = a < A$, lyrical poetry is directed primarily toward cognition of personal life, and this becomes an apperception of self-cognition. But inasmuch as *praesens* "is but a constantly generated and disappearing moment,"[37] the apperception of apperception, in order to become lyrical poetry, must be rendered as a "sign of previous thought," as a creative introspection whereby an unknown part of our mind becomes evident to us. It differs from epic poetry in that it recedes less into the past. It is subjective presence.

Dramatic poetry—comedy, tragedy, and tragicomedy—in contrast to epic and lyric modes, has no narrator or mediator between viewer and event. In it action is fused synchronically with its language,

---

[31] Potebnja, *Iz zapisok po teorii slovesnosti*, p. 532.
[32] Ibid.
[33] Ibid., p. 533.
[34] Ibid.
[35] Ibid., p. 531.
[36] Ibid.
[37] Ibid.

functions semiotically and constitutively. Both form syntactic series, and both generate complementary significations. Action as a metatextual semiosis lacks a determined external form; however, this does not mean that it is fortuitous. In order to function semiotically, it must form a "series or a chain whose links recede into the past and are retained in memory to the extent that the other [action] appears."[38] In other words, action, as an integral part of dramatic poetry, is to be arranged in a semantically meaningful text. Mime and dance, as pure dramatic action, represent such texts explicitly.

The paucity of Potebnja's remarks about epic, lyric, and dramatic forms may be explained by his belief that the psychological verisimilitude of the text is determined by the nature and function of its internal forms rather than by the norms extraneous to it. Consequently the epic, lyric, and dramatic forms of the poetic text are to be treated as less significant taxonomic markers. And yet this does not make them superfluous. A particular sonnet, for example, may have become an *ergon,* that is, may have lost its poetic potency, but as a poetic construct, nonetheless, must still be defined by the rules of its genre. Those rules or patterns, in Potebnja's view, must not be followed slavishly, because they might lead to sterile mannerism or pseudoclassical devices.[39]

From among various generic or intentional forms Potebnja chose the fable and the proverb as illustrations, believing that they could serve as models for such complex poetic works as the novel and novella, and such simple ones as a single poetic statement or even a word.[40]

The Fable

Potebnja's analysis of fable contended with that of G. E. Lessing (1729 – 81), a leading German theorist of the creative arts,[41] a classicist in literature, and rationalist in thought. One can even say that Potebnja's view of fable, in contrast to that of Lessing, is a *definitio*

---

[38] Ibid., p. 5.
[39] Ibid., p. 60.
[40] Potebnja, *Iz lekcij po teorii slovesnosti,* p. 1.
[41] Cf. G. E. Lessing's *Abhandlungen über die Fabel* (Vienna: Franz Prosch, 1867).

per contra. To Lessing, the fable was an application of universally valid maxims to particular existential events: If we were to reduce the general moral statement to a particular case and present it as actual— not as an example or comparison but as an instance that truly happened—and present it in such a manner that our narrative would explicitly facilitate the general assertion, then that work would be a fable. This definition was, no doubt, consonant with his belief in the aprioristic knowledge obtained independently of sensory experience. Potebnja, on the other hand, essentially an empiricist to whom experience was one of the presuppositions of knowledge, countered Lessing's definition:

> Thus before us there is a ready-made recipe from which one should conclude that first there exists the general moral confirmation in the mind, for example, 'flattery is harmful' or 'the mighty devours the weak,' and then for these we invent general statements—for the first, a fable about the crow and the fox, and for the second, that some wild animal ate up either a bird or some other animal and in turn was itself eaten up, and the like. Hence it follows that at first there is a general position that subsequently is reduced to a particular case or, as French theoreticians (De la Motte, Richer) say, disguises itself in allegory.[42]

"Fable," Potebnja went on to state, "cannot be (merely) the proof of one abstract statement because it serves as a focus of many abstract statements. . . . In regard to abstraction, fable is an allegory."[43]

Potebnja chose to describe the fable rather than other generic forms, because for him it was highly representative of the structure of the work of poetic art in general. Moreover, by fable, he "wanted to show the difference between the fundamental forms of human thought—poetry and prose—and thereby to demonstrate that these are not merely some temporary forms of cognition that, with progress, can be discarded, but rather are constant and definitely interacting."[44] These forms, he observed, "are like eyes; we use them wholly unconsciously; we notice their difference only when a noted personal-

---

[42] Potebnja, *Iz lekcij po teorii slovesnosti,* pp. 48–49.
[43] Ibid., pp. 72–73.
[44] Ibid., p. 39.

ity senses an ability for one or the other.''[45] In other words, Potebnja, very much like his German mentors, searched in fable for those non-variables of human cognition which generate knowledge.

The fable, perhaps more explicitly than other, more complex literary forms, is a binomial construct. It "consists of two parts; the first part is subject to explanation, is not expressed by words, does not enter the fable directly, and hence in abstraction is easily omitted. It can be called the *subject* or *explenandum* (*ob''jasnjaemoe*). The second part, which we usually call fable, is the *explaining* (*ob''jasnjajuščee*) [and] to some extent, the *predicate*.''[46]

What are the functional properties of these two constituents? Let us begin by looking at the second. Fable, as the predicate, in order to function as the continuous explanation of the ever-new existential predicaments, must have four characteristics: 1) It must consist of a series of actions; 2) the actions must form a definite unity; 3) the actants must be recognized without description or explanation; 4) the images must refer to concrete and individual events. Here are some examples: "A widow had a hen that laid an egg every day. I'll try to give the bird some more barley; perhaps it will lay twice a day, the housewife thought. She did this. The hen, however, got fat and stopped laying eggs altogether." There are four functions in this story. In contrast to it, Turgenev's prose poem, "Necessitas-Vis-Libertas," depicting an old, blind, and raw-boned woman pushing a large blind woman who, in turn, pushes a tiny, slender little girl, has only one action, and is therefore an emblem rather than a fable or, as Turgenev himself called it, a bas-relief. Such emblematic, or single-action stories, Potebnja contended, can be better depicted by spatial arts, that is, by painting or sculpture.[47]

---

[45] Ibid.

[46] Ibid., p. 11.

[47] The emblematic fable developed out of the *ut pictura poesis* literature and reached its apex in the works of the Renaissance fabulist Gilles Corrozet (1516–1568). Initially, such a fable was a combination of picture and text, but in time the latter subsumed the former; however, the idea that the text is but a corresponding component of the visual image was retained. Cf. Barbara Tiemann, *Fabel und Emblem* (Munich: Wilhelm Fink Verlag, 1974). Corrozet's emblematic fable was but an actualization of the Horatian dictum *ut pictura poesis,* which Lessing, in his celebrated *Laokoon oder über die Grenzen der Malerei und Poesie* (Berlin: C. F. Voss, 1766), had subjected to a thorough analysis and rejected. Potebnja embraced

In Phaedrus's fable "Calvus et musca," a fly bit a bald man on the head. Instead of hitting the fly, the man hit and harmed himself. To this the fly responded, "For a light pinch you wanted to punish a tiny insect with death; but what happened was that you added abuse to offense." The man responded, "I can easily reconcile myself, because I had no abuse in mind, but I surely would like to kill you— most contemptible animal that enjoys drinking human blood—even if it means great pain to myself." "How can this fable," Potebnja asked, "serve as an answer to a specific question if it contains two disparate answers?"[48] Consisting of two thematically disjoined fables, it lacks the second characteristic, unity.

To have direct access to actants, the poet frequently uses animals in lieu of people. Thus, instead of a cunning man, the fable uses the fox, and instead of a greedy man, the ass. Within the context of collective (ethnic) consciousness (or, within the interpreting community), such substitutions are automatically comprehended. As in a chess game in which players know the role of the pieces, fables with animal actants require no supplementary information to arouse our empathy; on the contrary, more information would most likely prevent them from being effective.[49]

Potebnja illustrates this property with Nathan's parable from 2 Samuel:

And the Lord sent Nathan to David: and when he was come to him, he said to him: There were two men in one city, the one rich, and the other poor. The rich man had exceeding many sheep and oxen. But the poor man had nothing at all but one little ewe lamb, which he had bought and nourished and which had grown up in his house together with his children, eating of his bread, and drinking of his cup, and sleeping in his bosom: and it was unto him as a daughter. And when a certain stranger was come to the rich man, he spared to take of his own sheep

---

Lessing's position entirely. Poetry and painting, he contended, perceive the object in two different modes, the former in action and the latter in stasis. It is for this reason that he classified such texts as Turgenev's poetry in prose as emblems rather than as fables.

[48] Potebnja, *Iz lekcij po teorii slovesnosti*, p. 17.

[49] Potebnja, critical of La Fontaine and Krylov who, like Lessing, preferred informational detail, advocated conciseness and simplicity such as is found in Aesop's fables.

and oxen, to make a feast for that stranger, who was come to him, but took the poor man's ewe, and dressed it for the man that was come to him.

All the references in this parable are direct rather than impersonal pronominal or generalized subjects, actuating neither doubt nor disagreement. Instead of questioning the veracity of Nathan's story, "David's anger (was) exceedingly kindled against that man."

The poetic effectiveness of the fable as well as its historical duration depend upon these four characteristics. Without them its capacity to function as a general explicatory schema for a host of existential predicaments would be seriously impaired. In comparison with its *explenandum,* this schema is and ought to be considerably simpler and clearer.[50] Should, however, some of its components become incomprehensible due to the absence of the corresponding predicament in life, then and only then is it either altered by substitution or rendered poetically sterile.

Let us return now to the first constituent of the fable—the subject. In situations in which the image, (predicate) can be explicitly correlated with the appropriate event, or exigency, the subject "does not have to enter the fable directly and in abstraction can be easily omitted."[51] For example:

A husband and wife daydreamed about what they would do if they won two thousand dollars in a lottery. But as in all cases when each person has a different idea, they began quarreling and said caustic things to each other. At that moment, however, they recalled the reverie of a gypsy who said, "I will forge musical instruments, go to the bazaar, buy a heifer that will grow to a cow that will have a calf and we'll drink milk." Thereupon a gypsy child said, "And I will ride the calf." The gypsy hit the child. "Don't you ride it—you may break its back." The husband and wife . . . burst into laughter and ended their quarrel.[52]

In this fable "the action is palpable and important." When, on the other hand, there is no explicit correlation between the event and the fable, then the fable is in need of some general conclusion, which can

---

[50] Potebnja, *Iz lekcij po teorii slovesnosti,* p. 38.

[51] Ibid., p. 11.

[52] Ibid., p. 40.

be rendered in one of three ways: "one particular story explains another particular story; the story explains a well-known general proposition; or the fabulist resorts to both possibilities at the same time."[53]

The first way, usually a double fable—or, as Lessing called it, *zusammengesetzte Fabel*—is to explain event A by event B. Examples are Krylov's "The Wolf and the Little Mouse" and La Fontaine's "Coq et la perle." Often "such a comparison is a complete parallelism, in the sense that not only does the case of the second story correspond to the first, but each verse in the first half corresponds to a verse in the second half."[54]

In the second of the three ways, Potebnja stated, a general proposition is validated by a particular instance. If it were the reverse, as Lessing proposed, the fabulist would always have to make a valid generalization, a task that is neither possible nor necessary, because images of the fable, in order to retain their poetic capacity, must remain potentially polysemous, that is, must be able to generate varied generalizations.

The third approach is a combination of the general proposition and a double fable. An example is Krylov's adaptation of Aesop's fable, "The Peacock and the Crow." In it the relevance of fable A is enhanced both by fable B and by the general proposition. But even such a concerted effort to ascribe the fable in question to one specific proposition seldom encompasses its overall generative capacity. As in the first two approaches, the "proposed proposition" must remain posterior to its central image.

Regardless of how the general conclusion or proposition is rendered, in authentic fables it is always just a prosaic addendum to the poetic text. Fables with such addenda resemble complex works of art that combine the text with an explicit metatext.[55] These fables contain three distinct meanings: the denotative or extensional meaning of the

---

[53] Ibid., p. 41.

[54] Ibid., p. 45.

[55] Such addenda appear, for example, in Phaedrus's "Gragulus superbous et pavo": "Ne gloriari libeat alienis bonis, Suoque ut potius habitu vitam degere, Aesopus nobis hoc exemplum prodidit"; in "Vacca et Capella": "Numquam est fidelis cum potente societas; Testatur haec fabella propositum meum"; in "Passer ad Leporem Consiliator": "Sibi no cavere et aliis consilium dare, Stultum esse paucis ostendamus versibus."

story; the connotative or allegorical meaning of the story; and the generic, mostly axiological, meaning, offered either at the outset or at the conclusion of the story. Of the three, the first and third are given, and the second is usually supplied in the process of reading.

What relationship can exist among these three meanings? If, as Potebnja believed, the fable having a significatory function reflects the structural arrangement of the concurrent poetry and prose, then, as in scientific inquiry, the third or generic meaning should function as a verification of the first two. This, in Potebnja's view, is not and should not be the case. In the sciences, verification is the expansion (*razloženie*) of the general conclusion into the elements of which it is composed.[56] Hence, it is but a reverse process of induction. The ideal verification is the one that expands the given conclusion without any remainder. Such verification is possible when the expandable components are bare signals of transmission, devoid of any auxiliary meaning and thus can be computed quantitatively. Consequently, "perfect proof or verification is possible only in mathematics, within the limits of finite quantities, and in logic to the extent that it generalizes the mathematical way of thinking."[57] When, however, the given general conclusion consists of components that transcend it semantically, then either they relate to it arbitrarily or they yield additional conclusions.

Fables, functioning as verifications of general conclusions, as a rule have an approximate character. They are not and cannot be proofs of one abstract proposition, because they always prove more than is necessary. Verification of a strictly scientific character would destroy their allegorical nature. The signs or images that transmit their stories are but a "point around which facts are grouped [and] out of which a generalization results."[58] Fables are therefore more a comparison than a scientific verification. Their role is more synthetic than analytic. They "help us to acquire generalizations rather than to verify them."[59] They are "the means of cognitive generalization and are

[56] Potebnja, *Iz lekcij po teorii slovesnosti,* p. 60.
[57] Ibid., p. 62.
[58] Ibid., p. 74.
[59] Ibid., p. 75.

moral, and as such must precede rather than follow what they tend to attain."[60]

The Proverb

The proverb may be formed out of a condensed fable. Such a condensation might occur in one of two ways. First, the fable's two givens—the story and the generalization—are inverted, the latter retained *in toto* and the former either condensed considerably or abandoned altogether. Here, for example, is a Serbian condensed fable: "'It looks like they are short of water and wood,' said the donkey who was invited to a wedding." Second, the very story of the fable becomes the proverb. For example, "The dog lies on the hay; it does not eat it, but it prevents others from doing so."

Fables of this type can be further condensed to what is generally known as sayings (*pogovorki*), allegorical images consisting of one person, one quality, or one action, but never of all three. As unidimensional constructs, they stand to proverbs as emblems do to fables. All languages have various sayings that explicate poetically the issues of life's condition, quality, and action. Here are a few examples in Russian: "U nego mednoj posudy—krest da pugovica, a rogatoj skotiny—tarakan da žukovica" ("Of copper dishes he has but a cross and a button; and of horned cattle, but a cockroach and a unicorn beetle"). How stupid is he? "Iz-za ugla meškom prišiblen" ("As if clobbered with a sack"). How drunk is he? "P'jan, kak noč'," ("Drunk as the night"). And so on. Expressions like "na ruku" ("playing into one's hand"); "po nutru" ("to one's liking"); "vezet" ("to be in luck"); and many others are poetic by virtue of retaining imaginative quality.

In all such cases, considerably more than in fables, the mind must provide appropriate thoughts, memories, or knowledge to make the proverbs meaningful. An instantaneous response to them implies that they must lie just "beyond the threshold of consciousness."[61]

---

[60] Ibid., p. 80.

[61] Ibid., p. 91. Potebnja's metaphor of consciousness as a "narrow stage that accommodates only a limited number of sensory data that therefore must enter, pass, and exit" was borrowed from J. F. Herbart's intellectualistic psychology. Accord-

Fables are not the only genre that can be transformed into proverbs. More complex forms, such as the comedy, epic, novella, and novel, can just as well be condensed into just one sentence, one statement, or even one "syntactical unit,"[62] and thus became proverbs. "The process of condensation of the larger story into a proverb is a phenomenon of enormous importance for human thought; to the extent it is accessible to our observation, condensation [is] unique to it."[63] The process reduces a large body of intellectual data to a relatively small one and thus facilitates and accelerates its movement.[64] Should, however, the process result in the disappearance rather than in the substitution or summation of the larger cognitive mass by the lesser one in the reader's consciousness, the value of such works will be a negative one. Their cognitive efficacy is, therefore, proportional to their power "to reduce disparate phenomena to a relatively small number of signs or images, and thereby to increase the importance of intellectual complexes entering our consciousness."[65]

Fable and Proverb as Exempla of the Work
of Poetic Art in General

By the time Potebnja chose to discuss it, the fable as an intentional aesthetic form was already largely extinct. Its historical span (beginning perhaps with cuneiform texts and lasting several millennia) had, by the end of the eighteenth century, finally reached its end. Johann G. Herder, the ideologue and theoretician of *Sturm und Drang* and an avowed apologist of the fable, wrote in 1801: "Arrogant times debase everything; thus the great teacher of nature and educator of mankind,

---

ingly, various presentations (*Anschauungen*) are struggling to get onto this stage via inhibition of and interaction with one another. Potebnja, to be sure, considered this definition as only a poetic figure: "While saying *stage, threshold*, etc., we resort to a poetic form of cognition. We are content with this figurative expression only because we cannot find another one for the solution of the important question." Ibid.

[62] Ibid., p. 102.

[63] Ibid., p. 96.

[64] Ibid., p. 97.

[65] Ibid., p. 98.

the fable, has gradually become a gallant chatterer or a childish fairy tale."[66]

From the very inception of modern, literary sensibility in Russia in the eighteenth century, the fable was a major genre, favored by such leading writers as A. D. Kantemir, V. K. Tredjakovskij, and A. P. Sumarokov. It achieved the highest point of development with I. A. Krylov in the first half of the nineteenth century.

In addition to reasons already cited, it was the historical termination of the fable that may have prompted Potebnja to focus on it. Unlike the novel, for example, a genre long in arriving, the fable, by reaching its temporal *statis*, had become most suitable for description and analysis. As Potebnja himself said, it was primarily the formal homogeneity and perspicuity of its essential components that were heuristically valuable and worthy of analysis.

Defining fable as a constant answer or predicate to a continuously changing subject, Potebnja came to believe that it was indeed the paradigm of all possible works of poetic art. Complex literary works, such as the epic, novella, novel, and drama, "in order to become such an answer would have to recede from us as into the distance, their dimensions decreasing before our eyes, their details disappearing and only easily perceptible general outlines being retained."[67] In short, to be an effective "medium of cognition, generalization, and moral,"[68] these works would also have to become fables.

This view of the fable was in no way new. During the eighteenth century, when the fable had reached is apogee, neo-classical and romantic theorists treated it in a similar way. Charles Batteux, for example, in his *Beaux Arts réduits a un même principe* (1746), observed that fable is constructed and functions in the same way as epic and tragedy. At its center there is an action with a beginning, a conflict, and an end, that, in order to yield a proper moral, must be narrated appropriately. Fables, therefore, should be regarded as either miniature epics or miniature tragedies. Batteux, however, by insisting on the fable's didactic aim and on the preexistent abstract or general

---

[66] J. G. Herder, *Sämtliche Werke*, 33 vols. (Berlin: Bernhard Suphan, 1877–1913), 23:255.

[67] Potebnja, *Iz lekcij po teorii slovesnosti*, p. 23.

[68] Ibid., p. 80.

truth of which the fable is but an illustration, differed substantially from Potebnja.

The view of the fable held by Potebnja was closer to Herder than to Batteux. A century earlier Herder had regarded the fable as a "source, a miniature, of the great poetic genres, where most of the poetic rules are found in their original simplicity and, to a certain extent, in their original form."[69] In the essay "On Image, Poetry, and Fable" (1787), Herder defined poetry in a way that was destined to influence greatly the aesthetics of German romanticism, particularly that of Goethe and Humboldt. By contending that the human mind perennially creates rather than passively receives images of reality, he placed it in the center of artistic as well as scientific creativity. Reality, he proposed, is not simply imitated or reproduced, but ever newly created. The continual flow of images through the mind that expresses itself in a variety of verbal and visual images is poetry. In this sense, "our entire life is, so to speak, a poetics. . . . Hence it follows that our soul, as well as our speech, continuously allegorizes."[70]

The fable, like all poetry, according to Herder, emanates from man's natural need to have a sense of and control over the external and internal realities. It is therefore merely one of the creative modes he uses "to explain the changes of the universe, its becoming, existence, and extinction."[71]

Again, the apparent similarity between Herder's and Potebnja's views on poetry and fable ought not be considered peremptory. While for Herder rationalism and didacticism were an abomination of the human spirit, for Potebnja, the centrality of cognition, both in poetic and scientific works, was a matter of epistemological exigency. Poetry and science might be different in the devices they employ, he maintained, but they both "aim at introducing unity and completeness into the diversity of (our) sensory data; the difference between their means and results demands that these two trends of thought . . . support and complement each other."[72] For Herder and his fellow thinkers of a century earlier, such a view of poetry and science would have

---

[69] Herder, *Sämtliche Werke*, 2: 98.
[70] Ibid., 15: 526.
[71] Ibid., 15: 535.
[72] Potebnja, "Mysl' i jazyk," p. 193.

been anathema; for Potebnja, it served both as epistemological concept and as method.

From this we should not deduce that Potebnja was a rationalist of some sort—dogmatic, inneistic, or aprioristic. Essentially a Kantian, he believed that our knowledge of the phenomena of sensory perception contains generalities that function by means of a priori elements. This was a far cry from Herder's *Glaubensphilosophie,* which in matters of knowledge ascribed priority to feeling and belief. It is in this philosophical context that the similarity, and difference, between the two scholars is to be viewed.

The fable, as a literary genre that had endured over millennia only to finally, at the end of the eighteenth century, outwear its poetic vitality, represents most markedly, in Potebnja's opinion, the structural arrangement of the work of poetic art in general. Its external form objectivizes the artistic image; its internal form, or the sign of the image, intimates the content or idea; and its content, although not given textually, is provided by the apperceiving consciousness. All three are structural components *sui generis.* The discernment of these components is therefore a simultaneous discernment of poetic art as such.

In order to function optimally, the image, or the concatenation of images, stated earlier in the fable, must have four properties: they must represent a series of actions; they must be thematically unified; they must be free of excessive attribution; and they must address existentially tangible events or cases.

In addition to the above components, the fable can also contain a general proposition or truth. Such a prosaic addendum, in Potebnja's view, does not and ought not to exist as the epistemological or axiological antecedent of the fable. "The role of the fable," Potebnja stated, "is synthetic. It helps us to acquire generalizations rather than to verify them."[73] In other words, the fable, within the limits of our experience, enlarges rather than simply confirms existing knowledge. In this respect, the fable, and in fact "all poetic works without exception,"[74] function as a focus for the diverse occurrences out of which emerges a general proposition or truth. Its structure can be represented by three concentric circles, of which *A* is the fable or the

---

[73] Potebnja, *Iz lekcij po teorii slovesnosti,* p. 75.
[74] Ibid., p. 80.

poetic text, *B* the occurrences or the existential context, and *C* the generalization or the prosaic addendum.

Conclusion

An eminent representative of Prague structuralism, Jan Mukařovský, wrote in 1934 in "A Note on the Czech Translation of Šklovskij's *Theory of Prose*" that Potebnja's school had "reduced the artistic aspect to something secondary, had rendered the work of art a passive reflection of something which was outside of art, had not differentiated sufficiently the specific function of poetic language from the function of the communicative utterance."[75] These imputations, clearly borrowed from Šklovskij,[76] were a misinterpretation of Potebnja's view of poetic form.

By "artistic aspect," Mukařovský meant the aesthetic orientation of the text toward the expression itself or toward its liberation from the referential, emotive, and connotative functions. If in poetic art a mode of utilizing the linguistic sign is indeed to free it from a unilateral bond with any of these functions, then Potebnja stands accused. If, on the other hand, one assumes, as Potebnja did, that due to the undifferentiable nature of the human mind, it is virtually impossible to break such a bond, and that any and all bondings of these functions are merely heuristic, then Šklovskij and Mukařovský's criticism are irrelevant.

It simply is not true that Potebnja "reduced the artistic aspect to something secondary." He found the dominant constituent of the poetic utterance to be its internal form, that is, such linguistically rendered attributes or their combination as are capable of invoking in the reader's perception completed objects or realities. In order to do this, these attributes or signs must be polysemous. The polysemy of the internal form, Potebnja observed, "is the property of poetic works."[77] The dissipation of this capacity automatically deprives these signs of their poeticalness and converts them into either communicative or referential signals.

[75] Mukařovský, *The Word and Verbal Art*, p. 135.
[76] Cf. V. Šklovskij, *O teorii prozy* (Moscow: Federacija, 1929), pp. 7–23.
[77] Potebnja, *Iz lekcij po teorii slovesnosti*, p. 139.

Even less plausible is Mukařovský's allegation that Potebnja's aesthetics "rendered the work of poetic art a passive reflection of something that was outside of art." This allegation bluntly contradicts Potebnja's fundamental claim that the work of art is *energeia* rather than *ergon*. As *energeia* it either continually creates new realities or explicates new questions of human existence. Passive reflection clearly purports either a structural analogy or a homology between the work of art and the intended reality. This is not the view Potebnja held. Poetic images or signs are metonymically organized systems, while intended realities, as they occur in consciousness, are often loosely organized aggregates. It is out of these aggregates, by means of apperception, that these signs form cognitive objects. There is an explicit disproportion between the two: in Potebnja's notation their relation is $a < A$. Metaphorically, they stand to each other "as alcohol and sugar stand to grain, potato, and sugar beets."[78]

Looking at Mukařovský's allegation from the standpoint of classical logic, passive reflection would also imply that the "reflected something" performs a validity function, and that aesthetic signs have a validity value. But to Potebnja, poetry, in relation to everything "that is outside of it" is untrue, while immanently it is true to itself. Humboldt put it even more directly: "The realm of imagination is directly opposed to the realm of reality; and equally opposed is the character of whatever belongs to one of these realms to anything within the other." Poetic art is "wholly opposed to reality."[79]

As for the last allegation—that Potebnja did not discern a specific function of poetic language—it can be said that his major effort, both in linguistics and in literary aesthetics, was to show how language, with manifest internal form, has always functioned either mythically or poetically, and conversely, with neutralized internal form, as an instrument of scientific reference.

To recapitulate: The work of poetic art is a "form of forms," a configuration of intentional and immanent forms. The former, inherently tied with man's progressing or regressing consciousness, specifies either its "poeticalness" or its "prosaicalness," the latter tied with historical conventions—its generic modification. This interconnection of mind and history, as it manifests itself in language, is a

---

[78] Potebnja, *Iz zapisok po teorii slovesnosti*, p. 65.
[79] Humboldt, "Über Goethes *Hermann und Dorothea*," p. 128.

constant reservoir of a never-ceasing creative quest, both poetic and prosaic. Primordially, from it there developed preflexional words and, subsequently, syntactically structured language, collective or folk creations, imaginative and realistic poetry, and mythic and scientific explications of spiritual and physical realities. All these forms represent a creative reciprocity between man and himself, man and men, and man and nature. In spite of their historical and synchronic peculiarities, they are similar in that all are narrative sequences, all function in accordance with specific rules, and all are directed toward some goal. Even though historically these forms are sequential to each other and thus could be distributed on a hypothetical axis from X to Y, they in no way invalidate one another. Their progression from imaginative to strictly referential functions, on the one hand, and their perseverance in both poetical and prosaic functions, on the other, are not mutually exclusive, inasmuch as language, of which these forms are the constituents, does not remain the same. Language, in its perennial variation, remains polysemous and thereby multifunctional. On the contrary, the two seemingly exclusive directions of language—poetry and prose—are complementary. Poetry, myth, and science, therefore, coexist in a state of symbiosis.

The difference between them lies in the manner in which their structural components—external form, internal form or images, and signification—relate to one another, or more precisely, how this relationship is perceived, both collectively and individually. In works of poetic art, images invoke signification and then dissipate without becoming a part of it; in myth, they are transferred into it; and in science, they remain neutral. Algorithmically, poetry, myth, and science represent three variant relations of X, a, and A, i.e., of X, a signification that is being sought, of a, an image by means of which signification is being sought, and of A, the aggregate of the previously acquired knowledge pertinent to X.

Intentional forms, unlike immanent ones (traditionally labeled as epic, lyric, and dramatic), depend entirely upon the authority of the existing convention. It is this authority that either affects or minimizes their heuristic power. Of the many variants of these three categories, Potebnja described in detail only the fable and the proverb, believing that these two best illustrate the nature and function of poetic works in general.

If we were to offer a criticism of Potebnja's theory of literary forms, ours, unlike that of Šklovskij and Mukařovský, would concern his inadequate attention to the external form. His only qualification for it was that external form should be "significant in its constitutive parts,"[80] and that it ought not impede the cognitive function of the internal form. That restrictive qualification considerably limits the aesthetic search for original arrangements and experimentation, for bold challenges to the existing forms of expression, and for what Umberto Eco called aesthetically overcoded constructs. The fable might indeed represent a group of generic variants, but it does not and cannot represent the entire spectrum of aesthetic possibilities. No literary genre can subsume all possible poetic variations. Behind all of Potebnja's formulations, there is the conviction that ultimately poetic art, like all other intellectual endeavors, must assist us in comprehending our existential predicaments, must expand our knowledge of ourselves and others, and must lessen intersubjective conflicts. These are, of course, noble goals, and poetry must not circumvent them—yet, they are not the exclusive ones. In "Preliminary Remarks about L. N. Tolstoj's and F. M. Dostoevskij's Art," Potebnja wrote: "If we were to suppose that reason, theory, and conscious striving toward some goal play no role in life, then we would destroy the possibility of discerning man's conscious life from the unconscious one."[81] Paraphrasing this remark, we can say that if we were to regard reason, theory, and conscious striving as the only source and regulator of poetic creativity, we would restrict it considerably and perhaps destroy it.

---

[80] Potebnja, *Iz zapisok po teorii slovesnosti,* p. 30.

[81] Potebnja, "Černovye zametki o tvorčestve L. N. Tolstogo i F. M. Dostoevskogo," in *Èstetika i poètika,* p. 561.

CHAPTER FOUR

Functional Determination
of the Work of Poetic Art

The Teleology of Poetic Images

Potebnja's algorithmic formulation of the work of poetic art, $X = a < A$, which he believed to be of general applicability, stipulates: first, that ontologically, such a work is a heteronomous construct insofar as the values of its members X and A are determined by disparate perceptive acts; second, that the formal constancy of a, as the only given of this formulation, yields disproportional and variable semantic correspondences; and third, that despite its mathematical expression, this formulation is contingent upon historical and psychological evidence rather than upon a strictly axiomatic truth. As such, therefore, it is not a pure deductive formulation. Given these inferences, it is appropriate and indeed necessary to treat a as a purposive member of the formulation and thus establish its relation to history and psychology.

Potebnja, in his three major works on literary theory, did not give this issue as much attention as it merited. His continuous references to the intentional nature of poetic art clearly point, however, not only to his keen awareness of it, but also to his conviction that poetic art is to be comprehended and appreciated in terms of its effect upon the perceiving consciousness. His very definition of it, as *energeia,* gains meaning because it is the efficient cause of something.

This, of course, does not mean that the work of poetic art cannot be isolated from these effects and considered only as a pure linguistic construct with a generative potentiality. Such an undertaking is complex because, as Potebnja observed, unlike an object of scientific inquiry, which, under laboratory conditions can be isolated from the start and reduced to a particular phenomenon, poetic art exists in history.[1] Nevertheless, in a manner of speaking, it can be lifted out of its historical context, bracketed, and reflected upon as an image or a set of images with potentially varied aesthetic and cognitive functions.

The teleology of *a* would pose less of a problem if *a* stood for a clearly definable object, be it observed, remembered, imagined, or reasoned—if it could be located in a clearly definable time and space. However, *a*, as has been shown, is a series of signifiers with no definite, and thus predictable, semantic correlates. It is pure form, which can, but not necessarily ought to, refer to this or that; yet whenever it does, it must be created anew. Therefore its ontology and teleology are coextensive, or, as Potebnja stated, the "categories of goal and means, by coinciding in all attributes, cannot be distinguished."[2] Every time *a* is used, it is born anew. Its "fixity by visible signs is not [its] true existence, but merely a means for [its] reproduction."[3] The poetic image, it follows, is as much an object as it is a medium to affect such an object.[4]

The teleology of *a*, we can infer, unlike that of the explicitly correlated signifier/signified, is difficult to establish. The poetic image, semantically multivalent or polysemous, can, and frequently does, refer to a series of mutually exclusive objects and can invoke multiple experiences and responses. Its relation to *X* can thereby be posited only in terms of probability. But as such, given a sufficient quantitative expression, it can be described generically, as it has been by Potebnja. Descriptively, in his view, the work of poetic art invokes varied psychological, fictive, and historical realities; inspires varied emotional and intellectual responses and innate dispositions; provides

---

[1] Potebnja, *Iz lekcij po teorii slovesnosti*, p. 4.

[2] Potebnja, *Iz zapisok po teorii slovesnosti*, p. 4.

[3] Ibid., p. 4.

[4] Formalists and structuralists, notably Šklovskij and Mukařovský, have criticized Potebnja for his inattentiveness to the specific properties of poetic designation, which, in their view, constitute the *differentia specifica* of poetic art. Potebnja, it is true, did not single out this aspect as being central to the poetic text, but he certainly did not ignore it. As the above definition indicates, the importance of the image in no way diminishes in active semiosis; on the contrary, it is enhanced. The image dominates the perceiver's attention even after it has actualized itself through the specific signified. To use Karl Bühler's schema, in aesthetic semiosis, the image, while it summons attention to itself, continues to be presentational, expressive, and appellative. In Potebnja's theory, these functions, are not mutually exclusive.

a focal point for both the poet's and the reader's mental aggregates; facilitates the formation of judgments and values; induces self-knowledge and emotional quiescence; objectivizes and transforms primary data of consciousness into well-composed wholes; and promotes the formation of general inferences.

Of course, these functions,[5] given the broad spectrum of psychological differences among creators and readers, can be expanded considerably. On the other hand, by involving the same faculties of mind, cognition, emotion, and conation, they can also be reduced to three generic categories: cognitive, expressive, and representational. In Potebnja's theory, unlike in psychoanalytic, structural, and semiotic theories, these functions are equipollent. Accordingly, a work of poetic art, because of the mind's unity, does not function cognitively without also affecting two other mental faculties. Quoting Hermann Lotze, Potebnja observed: "The mind (*duša*) manifests itself in these capacities not in parts; not with some of its parts awake and others still asleep. On the contrary, in each form of its activity it functions as a whole."[6] Hence, "it would be a mistake to consider cognition, emotion, and conation as completely independent."[7]

This functional syncretism does not preclude various ratios among the three. Depending upon the conditions under which these "capacities" (*sposobnosti*) are manifested, and the object toward which they are directed, their ratios can differ considerably, while their unity (barring, of course, pathology) remains constant. Consequently, a view that the work of poetic art generates only emotional catharsis, invokes only the sense of beauty or repulsion, arouses only a will to act, and the like, is, from Potebnja's perspective, explicitly reductive.

---

[5] Recently, such scholars as R. B. Braithwaite, A. Hofstadler, E. Nagel, and R. B. Perry, to name a few, have distinguished between purpose and function, or action. The latter, in their view, can also be nonteleological. Applied to works of creative art, such a distinction would imply that all or only some such works are goal-oriented. Potebnja, judging by the following statement, seemed to profess a similar view: "Works of art, emerging out of some artist's quest, complete this quest and thereby serve as its goal. Hence the question is not whether there are or are not external goals. The distinction between goal and action is beyond dispute. Action, its influence, if it is perceived, cannot be doubted, regardless of whether the artistic work had or did not have any such goal." *Iz zapisok po teorii slovesnosti*, p. 353.

[6] Potebnja. "Mysl' i jazyk," p. 82.

[7] Ibid., p. 80.

Speaking about the merits and shortcomings of Herbart's psychology, which claimed to apprehend the regularity of mental life as a whole, Potebnja asked: "Can this mechanism explain everything? Does not the parallelogram of mental powers contain a quantity that to us is both undefined and undefinable?" Hence—and this also applies to the problem of functions—"attempts to reduce everything to a single entity, no matter what, lead to a temptation unconsciously to remove something from a given set of facts so that we may explain the rest with less difficulty."[8]

Still, the disproportionate manifestation of the mental "capacities" in aesthetic experiences, as well as the dictates of the systematic investigation and formulation of functions, justifies separate accounts of cognitive, expressive, and auxiliary functions of the work of poetic art.

Cognitive Function

To understand Potebnja's position on the role the work of poetic art performs in cognitive processes, be they apprehensive or comprehensive, it is necessary to examine first his view of the very apparatus of these processes.

Potebnja referred to this apparatus as mind, consciousness, or simply thought. Both conceptually and semantically, his views were Herbart's as revised by Hermann Lotze, Theodor Waitz, and Moritz Drobisch. Accordingly, mind (*duša*) a simple spaceless essence or reality, is the sum total of presentations that arise in it on account of its contacts with other realities and that, after being positioned in it in accordance with their respective relevance, are in perpetual opposition, reciprocity, and reinforcement. Thus, presentations of the same sort but of greater force (for example, red versus green) move into the center of this configuration, while those with lesser force move either into periphery or below its threshold. Those representations which remain within the circumference of the configuration become elements of consciousness; those which fail become elements of subconsciousness. The latter, however, are subject to recall (*Hebung*) by

[8] Ibid., p. 79.

the appearance of new presentations similar to them. The rising of presentation, in turn, produces a vaulting (*Wölbung*) of all other arrested presentations that are similar to it.

Cognition is only an awareness of the relations among presentations. Retaining their qualitative uniqueness rather than fusing indiscriminately, presentations may be described mathematically. Knowledge, both perceptual and conceptual, is limited to relations. As Herbart said, we live amid relations and need nothing more.

Emotions and conations are also derivatives of specific arrangements of presentations. Rising, vaulting, opposing, and arresting among presentations generate a wide variety of feelings—emotions as well as desires. The will is only a variant of desire.

Herbart's schema, here intentionally reduced to its fundamental postulate, was further subjected by Potebnja to the following revision: Presentations, ideas, or complex images are mediated by language. On account of their spatial position in the mind, the strength of the accompanying emotions, the interest in them, the memory, and the intention, presentations enter into differential conjunctions. The center of the mind may accommodate more than one such conjunction simultaneously; it can function geometrically as well as sequentially. The simultaneity of two or more presentations in the center of the mind renders comparison, overall vision, and a sense of totality possible. Once transformed into syntactic constructions, however, presentations become narrative sequences. Through such constructions, space and time coalesce. Regardless of whether presentations are arranged spatially or sequentially, however, they are always integrated into some form of structure. "We are unable," Potebnja observed, "to imagine two impressions without imagining their being mutually related."[9] This structuring facilitates our mind's embracing larger quantities of presentations, for the ability to structure sensory data, thoughts, and impressions is expandable. Hence, "the higher the development of the mind (*duša*), the more refined are the relations by means of which it connects individual thoughts."[10]

The question of how the conjunction of two presentations generates signification, meaning, sense, and so forth is a complex one. The succession of presentations in mind, no matter how swift it may be,

[9] Ibid., p. 134.
[10] Ibid.

seldom explains their semantic linkage. Thus, for example, presentations *a* and *b,* succeeding one another, on their own strength may not
be able to yield any meaning. Therefore, any conjunction of presentations, in order to generate signification, must extend beyond their
immediate boundaries: must be related to the apperceptive mass, to
presentations beyond the threshold of consciousness. For this reason,
"in a moment when we are pronouncing the last word of the sentence,
we think directly only of the content of this word; however, this content points to what it refers to and from what it resulted—to all
preceding words of the same sentence, to the meaning of the paragraph, chapter, to the whole book."[11] This means, then, that some
"presentations that are already beyond the threshold of consciousness
have a more distinct influence on the cognized than others. . . . Each
member of the cognitive series introduces into consciousness the
results of all preceding ones. Hence, the more significant the result,
the more versatile are the connections among the preceding
members."[12] Without such an intricate interrelation, any series will
most likely be deprived of signification.

The basic rules of the cognitive series are those of association and
merging. In the former, "two discernible presentations, received
either simultaneously or sequentially, do not destroy their respective
independence," and in the latter they "are received as one."[13] The
new presentation, while merging with a previous one, inevitably either
underscores it or creates an incomprehensible mood. This merging,
however, will very likely involve other related presentations, thus
forming a bond that up to this time existed neither through simultaneity nor sequence.

Apperception and cognition, according to Potebnja (and in this he
differed from some of his German mentors, notably Lotze), as a rule
are formed by the complex union of three components, the perceived
(*vosprinimaemoe*), the explained (*ob''jasnjaemoe*), and the explaining
(*ob''jasnjajuščee*). "In apperception, the newly perceived and the
explained must, in a certain way, impinge upon the explaining.
Without [such continuity], there will be no result, no acquisition of the

[11] Ibid., p. 135.
[12] Ibid.
[13] Ibid., p. 136.

soul in which comprehension takes place.''[14] For example, when we ''say that or only sense that . . . we have recognized an acquaintance of ours by stature, walk, and dress, we admit that between the newly apperceived image of this acquaintance and the previously apperceived ones, there are common features—stature, walk, and dress.''[15] Without this ''means of apperception''[16] no explanation of the perceived could take place.

Functionally, as predicates, these ''means of apperception'' are not the object or the reality they invoke. They are configurations whose structure, $a + b + c$, may include the unknown x and y.

What then, in light of this schema of the human mind, is the cognitive function of the work of poetic art? In answering this question, Potebnja discerned two distinct, although related, issues—the creation and the perception of a work. In the first process, the work of poetic art functions as an evolving instrument of self-cognition. Prior to its manifestation, it exists as a possibility, as a cognition without the cognized, feeling without the felt, and willing without the willed. It exists in the poet's mind as a potential whole, and as an actual given, originates out of the aggregate of its presentations. ''We cannot imagine,'' Potebnja wrote, ''creativity out of nothing. Everything that man does is transformation of the existent.''[17] ''Out of the depth of his mind presentations arise, fuse, move in succession, and form marvelous images or abstract concepts, and all this occurs by itself, much like the rising and setting of heavenly bodies without the kind of mover that is necessary in a puppet show.''[18] This creative conjunction of presentations in the creative process is precipitated by a query, an X, in the poet's mind. The work that eventually emerges out of this

[14] Ibid.

[15] Ibid.

[16] Potebnja gave the following examples of how ''such means'' function. In Gogol's *Dead Souls*, Čičikov, the protagonist, speculates about the list of deceased ''souls'': ''Maksim Teljatnikov, a cobbler, Ux, a cobbler! Drunk as a cobbler, says the proverb; and then follows a typical story about a competition between a Russian cobbler and a German that explains the presentation of Teljatnikov. Here, part of the means [of apperception] is the fact that the surname that is being explained implies a calf-skin, and part is the presentation of a cobbler that follows it.'' ''Mysl' i jazyk,'' p. 137.

[17] Potebnja, *Iz lekcij po teorii slovesnosti*, p. 129.

[18] Potebnja, ''Mysl' i jazyk,'' p. 76.

conjunction is essentially a transformation of what has existed prior to its aesthetic objectivization. Ideally, the work should satisfy this query; in practice, however, "certain *X,* certain questions that disturb the writer, are clarified not by one cognitive act but by a series of works, a series . . . of answers that, as it progresses toward its conclusion, grows clearer and more definite."[19]

Self-cognition, according to Potebnja, is an awareness of that content of the mind which lies beyond its threshold, rather than an awareness of the cognizing mind itself. The former, as an object, is definable and accessible to us; the latter, as a subject, is not. Any definition of the cognizing mind turns it into the content or the object of thought. "The self-cognizing *I,* at least by our standards, is invariable, imperfectible, because we do not know the predicates by which such a change occurs."[20] Potebnja, very early in his studies, and as if anticipating William James and the phenomenological psychologists, distinguished the pure *I* from the empirical *I.* However, unlike them, he was hesitant to imbue the pure *I,* "this internal eye that intermittently turns toward and away from the stage of mental (*duševnaja*) life,"[21] with the regulating role. To him, "the apperceiving was not an invariable, pure *I,* but, on the contrary, something very variable [and] increasing along with our general development."[22] It follows, therefore, that it is the empirical *I* alone that functions both as the apperceiving and the apperceived rather than, as phenomenology holds, that the latter function is performed by the transcendental. "In self-cognition," Potebnja wrote, "the mind does not split into the *cognized* and the pure *cognizing I,* but passes from one thought to a thought about that thought—to another thought exactly like it in comparison, from the compared to what is being compared."[23] The only difference between the two components of this process is temporal: the cognized is past and the cognizing is present. "By saying," Potebnja observed, "that in the process of self-consciousness the cognized is past, we thereby approach its relation with the cognizing *I,* which is similar to what we do while reading, when two parts of a

[19] Potebnja, *Iz lekcij po teorii slovesnosti,* p. 146.
[20] Potebnja, "Mysl' i jazyk," p. 168.
[21] Ibid., p. 168.
[22] Ibid., p. 169.
[23] Ibid.

sentence, one completed and the other just being read, complement each other and fuse into one act of thought."[24] In brief, the entire process of self-cognition, in terms of the above schema, occurs between the mind's center and its periphery rather than by the two coextensive selfs.

Self-cognition through poetic creation is a dynamic act of self-retrospection. As such, it differs from the passive reflection of past experiences, in that it is a demonstrated reproduction of the mind's presentations through linguistically structured forms. Through them the poet seeks to recover his past experiences, dreams, and anxieties, and thus to come to know himself. But, like all endeavors involving the inner recesses of mind, the creation of poetic art can, in facilitating such knowledge, at the same time impede it. Humboldt's axiom that each understanding is at the same time a non-understanding, and that each agreement in thoughts and feelings is likewise a disagreement, is, according to Potebnja, as valid here as it is in other modes of linguistic definitions.[25] Works of poetic art should in no way be considered as definitive statements about the poet's mind. None of the images he creates define his X conclusively. "We can say," Potebnja stated, "that the X of the poet is inexpressible, that what we call expression is only a series of attempts to define this X rather than to express it. It is

---

[24] Ibid.

[25] There is an abundance of poetic statements to the effect that poetry also inhibits self-cognition. Potebnja cites (*Èstetika i poètika,* pp. 558–59) two well-known examples from Russian literature, one by Lermontov, entitled "Don't Trust Yourself" ("Ne ver' sebe") and another by Tjutčev, entitled "Silentium," the second stanza of which reads:

> Как сердцу высказать себя?
> Другому как понять тебя?
> Поймет ли он, чем ты живешь?
> Мысль изреченная есть ложь;
> Взрывая, возмутишь ключи,—
> Питайся ими—и молчи.

> How will the heart express itself?
> How will another understand you?
> Will he understand what it is that you live by?
> A thought that is spoken is a falsehood.
> By stirring up the springs you will cloud them.
> Drink of them—and be silent.

like having a candle in front of us that provides light. Do we exhaust the entire essence of what is before us by this single signification of 'candle'? Evidently, one poetic image does not express this X."[26]

As to the cognitive function in the perception of the work of art, Potebnja observed:

> The process of comprehension of the word and the poetic image is completely analogous to the process of their creation; when we comprehend the spoken word or the poetic work, we experience the same three elements, only in inverse order. In creating the poetic work, at the moment when X is being explained by means of A, a emerges. In comprehending it, the listener or the reader is first given only a sign—a; but this sign must be explained by the reserves of our previous thought—by A. We can comprehend poetic work to the extent we can participate in its creation.[27]

The inverted correspondence, then, is $X = a < A \equiv a < A = X$.

This correspondence should not be taken as semantically coextensive, however, because comprehension of the work of poetic art is not a mere "transfer of the content from one head to another."[28] It takes place as a function of the "identical structure of human thought,"[29] rather than as a function of the thought itself. Moreover, out of the three elements involved in both processes, only a is constant, where X and A are variables; hence, it is logical to assume that a paired measure like this will vary in accordance with the value of the two variables. As indicated, such measures cannot function inductively inasmuch as their members are not bare signals of transmission. The work of poetic art, it follows, in spite of the structural correspondence between artistic creation and aesthetic perception, is an ever-new semantic transformation of its imagery.

In what sense, then, does the work of poetic art affect the cognitive faculty of its reader? The answer is contained in the above equation. First, the reader cognizes those thoughts of his mind which are "unor-

[26] Potebnja, "Mysl' i jazyk," p. 169.
[27] Potebnja, *Iz lekcij po teorii slovesnosti*, p. 136.
[28] Ibid.
[29] Ibid.

ganized and uncrystallized.''[30] Without such thoughts, represented in it by *A*, cognition could not take place. The cognition of *a*, therefore, is conditioned by its semantic correlate in *A*; hence the reader learns what he is predisposed to learn. For example, many elements of the fictional or dramatic plot, in order to be apperceived, must be consciously or subconsciously familiar to the reader. Without this antecedent "knowledge," the work in question would be inaccessible and therefore either rejected or ignored. Without this affinity, which is attested to during aesthetic perception, the work of poetic art would cease to exist. Potebnja observed: "The processes that are occurring in [the poet's] mind, to the extent we can know them, are of great interest because essentially they are the processes of our mind, the mind of those who comprehend and use works of poetic art. The poet's personality is exclusive only because its elements are more concentrated than the elements of those who understand his works. Between the poet and the audience of his time there exists a tight bond that periodically expresses itself in facts of great sensibility.''[31]

The cognitive function of the work of poetic art extends also to realities beyond the perceiving mind. The apprehension of these realities occurs through and by the actualities of that mind, and therefore it, too, appears as a kind of *connaissance de soi*. Potebnja wrote: "In a broad and at the same time strict sense, all properties of the mind are subjective—even though they are conditioned by the external world, they are still the product of personal creation. In this all-encompassing subjectivism, however, one can discern the objective and subjective, and can ascribe science to the former and art to the latter.''[32]

In what way can we apprehend the reality around us through poetic works? Potebnja gives a qualified answer to this question. Creative arts in general, and poetic art in particular, do not and cannot simulate or reproduce life, reality, or nature apart from the very psychological processes that engender their imaginative or conceptual configurations. "Generally," he wrote, "everything that we call the world, nature, what we posit outside of ourselves, as a totality of objects and reality, including our own *I*, is but a plexus of our mental

[30] Ibid., 137.
[31] Ibid.
[32] Potebnja, "Mysl' i jazyk," p. 195.

processes, even though not fortuitous but conditioned by something outside us."[33] To become conscious reality, this plexus needs language and thought. Once rendered imaginatively or conceptually, it is no longer "the raw material,"[34] but a phenomenon of our mind. Hence, creative arts, as particular transformations of such "materials," are not and cannot be mimetic. Poetry, Potebnja wrote, "like science, is the explanation of reality, its elaboration for the sake of the new, more complex, and higher goals of life."[35] It is ideal in the sense that its imagery is singled out from the primary complex of percepts, that it coalesces one set of presentations and eliminates those which might hinder the thought. On the one hand it is "truncated"; on the other, comprehensive. Its central image or concatenation of images expresses a certain perspective, a point of view, and seldom, if ever, the essence or *noema* of reality. By ascribing a dominant position to one attribute of reality, poetic art remains but a subjective endeavor to create sense out of the never-ceasing flow of percepts, an ever-new attempt to know the unknowable.

The limited and transformed reality that emerges out of aesthetic cognition is in no way superfluous or inferior to that of scientific reconstruction. First, it plays a vital role in the preconceptual processes of the mind, inasmuch as it unifies its sensory representations into cognitive wholes without insisting on their logical or empirical verification. Second, and this is somewhat paradoxical, it generates the sense of unity while itself it is but a partial representation of it. Third, "in some way, it compensates for the imperfection of scientific thought, and satisfies man's innate need to see completion and perfection everywhere, thus not only paving the way for science, but, temporarily, arranging and completing its low-lying edifice."[36] Fourth, by inviting the perceiver to partake in the creation of imaginative reality, poetic cognition is genuinely convergent, because in one and the same work it can accord equal credence and validity to both imaginative and objective renditions of reality and thus neither deny nor minimize the creative role of the perceiver. Stripped of such a

[33] Potebnja, *Iz zapisok po teorii slovesnosti,* p. 65.
[34] Ibid.
[35] Ibid., p. 67.
[36] Potebnja, "Mysl' i jazyk," p. 194.

role, the work of poetic art could not exist; its structure is impossible without its ever-new reconstruction.

Expressive Function

If the three members of Potebnja's equation—*X, a,* and *A* —were to denote only the cognitive data of our mind, without affective and conative concomitants, then very likely they could be read merely as denotative markers of one class of phenomena. In that case, the poetic text would be unifunctional; however, we know that *A* represents an aggregate of dynamic presentations that, while opposing, arresting, reinforcing, rising, vaulting, and arching, become charged affectively and conatively. For example, a presentation *B,* while rising from below the threshold of mind, might be impeded or reinforced by presentations *D* and *E* and thereby accompanied by the opposite qualities. From this one is to conclude that *X, a,* and *A* are multivalued and multifunctional. Reading a poem or a novel, viewing a dramatic performance, listening to a recital, and the like are not and cannot be purely intellectual acts whereby the perceiver, by means of a subjective arrangement of poetic images, gains nothing but knowledge of himself and others. Instead, all such acts are complex involvements with poetic texts that, in addition to cognition, excite and alleviate diverse emotions and serve a variety of didactic and heuristic ends.

Potebnja, much like his German mentors, believed that the poetic text "excites the whole man,"[37] exerts "power over his heart," and "purifies his thoughts and emotions."[38] These cathartic effects, he added, do not and should not occur in isolation from cognition and conation, because the nondiscriminable response is not its goal. Such a response would be deviant, if only because of its inconsistency with the syncretic nature of the mind. Art, he cautioned, ought not to cause excitement, anxiety, or agitation without at the same time alleviating such experiences through cognition. Its aim must be, by means of images, "to decompose and destroy the power of disturbing emotions, to push them into the past," and thereby "to purify and simplify the

[37] Ibid., p. 189.
[38] Ibid.

thought.''[39] Quoting Humboldt, Potebnja wrote that the ancients best exemplified such psychologically balanced art:

> While reading the ancients, a well-tuned soul experiences quiescence. Thanks to it the ancients either reduce passionate agitation and overpowering despair to spiritual quiescence, or elevate it to courage. This strength-inspiring quiescence occurs inevitably after man has reviewed his relation to the world and to his destiny. When, however, either the external power or his own passion threatens to disturb this equilibrium, he experiences aggravation and despair (*verzweifelnder Missmuth*). In the scheme of things, however, it happens that as soon as he completes the full circle of phenomena, presented to him by fantasy in serious moments of his reckoning with his destiny (*in diesen Augenblicken einer ernsten Rührung*), harmony and quiescence are restored immediately.[40]

The expression of affective concomitants in the creation process is usually induced by a conjunction of presentations that contains an unknown, ambiguous, or inconsistent element: an X. Such a conjunction, while being completed, might be accompanied by a variety of hindering experiences, such as exaggerated restlessness, alteration of despair and hope, and the like. This X, regardless of its complexity, is described by Potebnja as follows: ''Something (X) that is vague to the author appears to him as a question. He can find the answer [to it] only in his memory, in its acquired or in its intentionally broadened content (A). Speaking figuratively, . . . in this A, under the influence of the question X (''what?''), there emerges some anxiety, movement, agitation; from A, X repulses everything unsuitable and attracts everything that is related to it. The latter crystallizes itself into an image a, being comprised of the floating elements. Thus a judgment, $X = a$ (from A), as well as the quiescence that completes the evolving act, is affected.''[41] It follows that, until the completion of the creative process, or until the occurrence of such judgment, X generates a state of tension. Potebnja wrote: ''The more persistent the question, the more anxious the pangs of the emerging thought, and the greater the desire to calm one's emotions and to clarify the thought, . . . the more perfect

[39] Ibid., p. 190.
[40] Ibid., p. 189.
[41] Potebnja, *Iz zapisok po teorii slovesnosti*, p. 32.

and pleasing will be his work to others.''[42] This, Potebnja stated, has been confirmed by a great many poets. For example, Mixail Lermontov, in the poem "Fairytale for Children" ("Skazka dlja detej"), wrote:

> Этот дикий бред
> Преследовал мой разум много лет,
> Но я, расставшись с прочими мечтами,
> От него отделался стихами.

> This wild delirium
> Persecuted my mind for many years;
> But I, parting with other daydreams,
> Have gotten rid of it by my poems.

However, because one creative act can seldom define this X conclusively, or to put it formally, because a single $a < A$ hardly equals X, the cognitive quiescence, too, is relative. Hence, Lermontov could get rid of the "wild delirium" only by *poems* rather than a particular poem. Works of poetic art, while transforming this X into meaningful propositions, often provoke additional questions and thereby lead to protracted despair and a conviction that there are no adequate resolutions to existential predicaments. Poetic works, then, accentuate rather than alleviate discord, dejection, and feelings of inadequacy.

In aesthetic perception, the convergence of $X \rightarrow a$ may be outlined as follows: In apprehension of the work of poetic art, X, instead of being antecedent, is subsequent to a. In Potebnja's words, "apprehension is a repetition of the creative process in an inverted order."[43] Translated into psychological terms this statement infers that, correspondingly, the two X's in the perceptive and the creative processes act as supraliminal and liminal, or subliminal, stimuli. However, in Potebnja's view, such works are irrelevant, inasmuch as their images are semantically unproductive. As he put it, "without image, there is no art, and particularly there is no poetry. Without complexity (*mnogosložnost'*), concreteness, there is no image. Art of all times directs [our] efforts toward the acquisition of the internal goal. A certain multiplicity of attributes and the durability of their

---

[42] Ibid.
[43] Potebnja, *Iz lekcij po teorii slovesnosti,* p. 549.

cohesion—the facility with which it is apprehended and retained by those who understand it—is the measure of its artistic value."[44] Poetic images, as determinate stimuli, are to be apprehended readily.

The difference between the two stimuli, in terms of the response they elicit, can be considerable. In the creative process it can elicit anxiety, agitation, aggravation, despair, and, as Lermontov wrote, delirium. Any obscure or vaguely defined objects, events, queries, or the like that excite our receptors, or evoke our curiosity, or provoke us to act might indeed be accompanied by similar affective experiences. However—and here Potebnja was not sufficiently discriminative—once the X is given adequate verbal expression, as it is in the work of poetic art, emotional concomitants need not be of such extreme character, unless, of course, the perceiver confounds the signification of this work with extraliterary realities. The two X's might turn out to be dissimilar if only quantitatively. Affective concomitants, commonly known as aesthetics, are a distinct class of their own. For one thing, they are determined by the distribution, movement, and interrelationship of the actual images rather than, as in poetic creation, by the quest for such an image. For another, they are evaluative rather than purely expressive, and hence are subject to the limitation of aesthetic conventions or, as Hans R. Jauss aptly put it, to the "modalities of reception."[45]

Auxiliary Functions

By the above-mentioned functions of the work of poetic art, Potebnja did not contend (as, subsequently, symbolists, formalists, and structuralists did) that its ontology was to be conceived in terms of the specific roles it performs. His notion of "poeticalness" did not imply restricted functions and specific purposes. To Belyj (a symbolist), for example, art was "to penetrate into essences of phenomena"; to Šklovskij (a formalist), it was to enhance our perception of reality

---

[44] Potebnja, *Iz zapisok po teorii slovesnosti*, p. 83.

[45] Jauss distinguishes five levels of aesthetic identifications: associative, admiring, cathartic, sympathetic, and ironic. Cf. his "Negativität und Identifikation: Versuch zur Theorie der ästhetischen Erfahrung," in *Positionen der Negativität*, ed. H. Weinrich (Munich: Wilhelm Fink Verlag, 1975), pp. 263–339.

or, metaphorically, "to make the stone stony"; to Mukařovský (a structuralist), art was to create semantic autonomy of its language through special designation. To Potebnja, it was to do all this and more.

The multifunctionality of the poetic text, in Potebnja's theory, was a logical outcome of his psycholinguistics. Once he defined language as energy that creates thought, forms our *Weltanschauung,* systematizes our internal presentations, and provides sense to our sensory perceptions—in short, regulates our relationship with ourselves and the world—he could not but regard it as central to our *entire* psychic constitution. Accordingly, for all our mental processes, language is indispensable. To him, as to his German mentors, without constant transformation and retransformation, affected by language, no imaginative representation, no conceptualization, and therefore no thinking, no feeling, and no willing, is possible. All these processes are but different operations of the same linguistic capacity.

The work of poetic art, as a linguistically dependent variable, is inevitably involved in all these processes. Therefore, to ascribe to it only one function would imply a radically different arrangement of these processes, as well as a structure of mind whose components can function in isolation rather than in causal dependence. This dependence of cognition, emotions, and conation, as shown previously, does not mean that discrimination among their functions is not warranted. In spite of their frequent simultaneity, their functions can still be arranged in an equiproportional table.

To Potebnja, the cognitive function was dominant, whereas the expressive, presentational, and axiological functions—inasmuch as they are elicited "by the way" rather than intentionally—were secondary. "Any poetic image, by means of its metaphoricity, in a narrow sense, or by its typicalness (that is, by cognition) can incidentally exert such an influence. On this basis, there is widespread conviction about the ethical, educational, and ennobling significance of poetry in general."[46] However, under certain conditions, poetic art, as well as art in general, has pursued only these secondary functions. In the past, "laudatory verse making" and, at present, the *littérature engagée* illustrate this point.

[46] Potebnja, *Iz zapisok po teorii slovesnosti,* p. 78.

The auxiliary or secondary functions, Potebnja alleged, are detrimental to the work of poetic art if and when they are considered the dominant ones. As shown in the case of the fable, the "ready recipe," or abstract ethical judgment, that exist prior to the poetic text are striking illustrations of this. When secondary functions are considered dominant, Potebnja insisted, poetic work is rendered prosaic, scholarly, or scientific. "If someone," he wrote, "decides in advance to prove or to persuade, and then consciously aims toward a definite goal, and proves by *example* what should have been proved, then he is a prose writer, scholar, moralist, preacher, or prophet, but not an artist. If, on the other hand, he, after having chosen an example, imparts it with vitality and concreteness, then inevitably it will say more, or even something entirely different, than what was intended. This way, under the influence of the artist's character, the didactic goal will become secondary."[47]

Auxiliary functions, however, need not be deleterious to poetic art. If the antecedent thesis does not distort the corresponding example, then the didactic work will have a worth equal to the poetic one. "In order to be a didacticist and a poet simultaneously, one must love truth, which will prevent the distortion of the example to the advantage of what has to be proved by it. Under such conditions, didactic poetry is equivalent to pure poetry. Its merit depends also on what has to be proved by it. This *demonstrandum* may be the image of the poet's character and the attitude of his mind. In this way, didactic poetry becomes subjective and, in a sense, lyrical. The author will speak through the protagonists of novels and dramas which, in turn, will become both lyrical and didactic."[48] In other words, for this *demonstrandum* to become a work of art, it must be congenial with the poet's imaginative vision. While remaining general, it must become genuinely personal. Moreover, no matter how compelling the objective reasons for its existence may be, the justification for its aesthetic being is subjective. Potebnja put it in yet a different way: "The process of creation (*energeia*) and the created (*ergon*) and the author's attitude toward one and the other are irreconcilable so long as they are

[47] Ibid., p. 83.
[48] Ibid.

looked upon as synchronic phenomena."[49] Their contradiction terminates once they are considered to be diachronic—as they indeed are.

Criticism as a Mode of Cognition

The following schema emerges from Potebnja's concept of poetic image and the few observations he made about the nature and function of criticism: As a process of knowing, criticism does not differ essentially from other types of scholarly cognition. In it the direction of thought proceeds from a (the given) through A (the previous knowledge) to X (the question to be answered). This cognitive course is similar to that found in any systematic scholarly scientific inquiry; however, the overall similarity does not describe the full dimension of criticism.

As a scientific cognition, Potebnja held that criticism is the act of reasoning from the particular fact to the corresponding rule (*zakon*) "that is invariable, static, determined, and which expresses itself uniformly in all related facts."[50] Generally speaking, there are three types of cognition—poetic, ordinary, and scientific. In poetic work, "the particular is [elucidated] by another heterogeneous particular";[51] in ordinary work, by subjective assumptions; and in scientific work, by the objectively binding rules. Hence, while every concerted reading of the poetic text is an act of cognition, not every reading is an act of criticism.

Criticism, thus defined, centers on what is actually given—on a rather than on any significations it generates, because such significations $(X_1, X_2, X_3, \ldots X_n)$ change every time they are apprehended. Moreover, raising one such signification to the level of definite reference would either contain the generative capacity of a or convert it to myth. The intended reference, X, "is indefinable, if only

---

[49] Ibid., p. 55.
[50] Ibid., p. 100.
[51] Ibid.

because, even to the poet himself, it is explicated only to the extent that it expresses itself through its image, that is—partially."[52]

The "facts" of criticism, it follows, are the external and internal forms of the poetic work. They alone are available and accessible to description and analysis. Specifically, criticism describes the "geneology of poetic images" in the same way that linguistics describes the etymology of internal forms of individual lexemes. Such a geneology can be established within the creative scope of one author, a group of authors, a literary period, trend, or even national literature. However, no matter how extensive this geneology might be historically or culturally, its focus must remain the author's creative mind, because in authentic works of art all poetic affinities, adaptations, imitations, and the like are, as a rule, mediated through its uniqueness. This fact in no way minimizes the importance of the collective consciousness in the geneology. Criticism must take heed of its effect on the geneological sequence of poetic images, but avoid stressing it as the major cause of their correspondence. In short, it must discern between subjective and collective factors as they condition the poetic process. An exclusive emphasis upon the former might easily lead to an erroneous view of poetic art as a phenomenon detached from its historical context; and on the latter, a denial of its individual authenticity. While it is true that "between the poet and the audience of his time there is a very tight bond that sometimes manifests itself in tangible results,"[53] that "his personality is exclusive only in the sense that it possesses in greater concentration those elements which his readers also possess,"[54] it is equally true that he creates for and out of himself. Translated into systematic methodology, such discernment ostensibly implies a polynomial definition of criticism. It is safe to conclude that criticism in terms of Potebnja's theory of literature, should, in its effort to explain the nature and origins of the poetic text, avail itself of history, psychology, linguistics, and cultural anthropology.

Finally, criticism must not remain oblivious to the effects of the poet's sense of artistic as well as extra-artistic obligations on his art. "Freedom of creativity," Potebnja wrote, "as freedom of conscience

---

[52] Ibid., p. 34.
[53] Potebnja, *Iz lekcij po teorii slovesnosti*, p. 137.
[54] Ibid.

in general, is the right that imposes obligations.''[55] ''The true artist, not a dilettante, not a speculator, by each act of his creativity, is solving an important problem for himself and, should his personality stand out among others, an important problem for his contemporaries.''[56] His conscious intercourse with his milieu, therefore, is bound to exert influence, or even determine his poetic perception and creativity. Hence, to be able to create historically credible and aesthetically valent works, he must be both ''inexorably truthful with his impressions,''[57] and free and educated in his views. In short, truth, freedom, and education, coupled with talent, enable him to seize life.[58]

These ''obligations,'' Potebnja qualified, must not function as antecedent, conscious formulations of the creative process, because as such, they would inevitably lead to its abstraction and ultimately to its stultification. Most of the time these ''obligations'' operate subliminally and concomitantly through introspection and observation. Poetic images, while subject to ''these obligations,'' nevertheless remain free from their deductive pressure. Otherwise they would be merely the dictates of the specific truth, axiom, or platitude. This makes them function as signs or symbols of the indeterminate series of the corresponding reality.

Criticism, while being well aware of these obligations, must nevertheless describe and evaluate works of poetic art only in terms of their aesthetic authenticity and their capacity to serve as predicates to ever-new subjects.

---

[55] Potebnja, *Iz zapisok po teorii slovesnosti*, p. 43.

[56] Ibid., p. 45.

[57] Ibid., p. 44.

[58] There are many examples of poetic art produced in Russia that lack one of these factors. In Potebnja's view, the works of the Slavophiles, for example, were written in the absence of freedom. As a result, Potebnja stated, their works turned out to be lifeless and produced through ''tinted glasses''; even Tolstoj's *War and Peace*, Potebnja alleged, reflects such a lack. ''The saddest example of the absence of true freedom, deriving from the absence of true knowledge, is Tolstoj's latest work (*War and Peace*), which, by virtue of its creative power and poetic gift, stands at the head of everything that appeared in European literature since 1840. No! . . . Without education, freedom in a broad sense—in regard to oneself, one's preconceived ideas and systems and even in regard to one's nation, one's history—we cannot imagine a true artist. Without this air, it is impossible to breathe.'' *Iz zapisok po teorii slovesnosti*, p. 44.

Potebnja, regretfully, did not engage in "applied" criticism, save numerous textual illustrations to his theoretical contentions. The longest of these illustrative digressions, although validating only one theoretical contention, was his attempt to determine the similarity between the X in Aleksandr Puškin's poem "Imitation of the Koran" ("Podražanie Koranu") and Mixail Lermontov's "Three Palms" ("Tri pal'my"). Potebnja contended that the formal similarities of these poems and the core of their imaginative nexus permit us to deduce that Lermontov, while wrestling with his X, most likely resorted to Puškin's "Imitation," which by that time must have been a part of his apperceptive mass, his A. Consequently, the X in both poems represents the gamut of sad feelings such as solitude, deprivation, and a quest for something that can no longer be recovered.

Juxtaposing "Three Palms" with other works Potebnja also inferred that the poem led Lermontov to further attempts to resolve the same X through *The Hero of Our Time* (*Geroj našego vremeni*) and *Princess Mary* (*Knjažna Mèri*). In short, Potebnja's synoptic account of the creative antecedents of Lermontov's works stipulates, first, that Puškin's "Imitation" actuated a cycle of Lermontov's poetic and narrative works; second, that all these works attended to the same poetic quest; and third, that in spite of the protracted attempts to resolve it, this quest remained unattainable.

Potebnja's "Preliminary Remarks about L. N. Tolstoj's and F. M. Dostoevskij's Art" reflects little of his literary aesthetic. His selections from *War and Peace* prove rather that Tolstoj's philosophy "was based on the unquestionable position that the phenomenon is inexhaustible by cognition, and hence its explanation can never be equal to it." From this assumption Potebnja inferred that Tolstoj had "contempt for reasoning, for theory and practice guided by theory."[59] It is obvious that Potebnja was irritated by Tolstoj's relentless assault on formalized knowledge, as expressed by science, jurisprudence, history, academic institutions, etc. Quoting *Le roman russe* (1888), he agreed with its author, E. M. Vogüé, that "Tolstoj, earlier and more than anybody else, was the expounder and disseminator of that condi-

---

[59] Potebnja, "Černovye zametki," p. 561.

tion of the Russian soul which was called nihilism."[60]

Potebnja's reading of Dostoevskij's *Diary of a Writer* (*Dnevnik pisatelja* 1876–1877), is hardly critical, even though at its very onset he admits that the "better part of the *Diary* is imaginative, poetic allegory" and that the "power of the artist lies in images and not in reflections in which he ceases to be the artist."[61] Logically, from this initial remark, which emphasizes the key contention of his theory, one would expect Potebnja to focus on the *Diary* as a poetic text. Yet, defying his own stipulation that the "definition of poetry must not include any references to the contents and the quality of the images,"[62] he does exactly that, focusing on its contents, which, in his view, was "confined to three issues: us (people of the educated society), ordinary people (*narod*), and Western Europe."[63] Perhaps our conclusion that his "Preliminary Remarks" conforms to Potebnja's critical theory is too harsh or even unjustified, because they were meant to be private[64] and as such they represent Potebnja as a reader rather than as a critic.

Conclusion

From the perspective of Western ideas on the telic nature of poetic art, Potebnja's position is neither novel nor revealing. Ideas of self-knowledge, the functional reciprocity between poetry and science, the expression of the emotions suffused with the formal structure of a work of art, poetically contained didacticism as primary and secondary aims—all have been postulated by Western aesthetics beginning with the classical Greeks. In the Russian Empire, however, these ideas, if only by their utter contrast to those of the conservative and radical critics, should have been recognized immediately; but they were not. They had to wait almost two decades before they were even

---

[60] Ibid., p. 565.

[61] Ibid., p. 577.

[62] Potebnja, *Iz zapisok po teorii slovesnosti*, p. 59.

[63] Potebnja, "Černovye zametki," p. 577.

[64] They appeared in *Voprosy teorii i psixologii tvorčestva*, vol. 5 (1914).

acknowledged by the symbolists as a "strong basis"[65] of their poetics. In the meantime, the Russian critical scene of the 1860s and 1870s was dominated by the ideologically charged demands of Černyševskij, Pisarev, and Dobroljubov that literature be an "auxiliary force" and propaganda. Potebnja's reaction to these demands, although explicitly restrained, was manifestly negative. He was particularly disturbed by these critics' total preoccupation with the extra-aesthetic functions of literature and characterized their condescending view of it with a fable about a pig, which, after having fed on acorns, proceeded to uproot the oak tree.[66]

At this point it is instructive to reverse the issue discussed in this chapter and ask how functions affect the very work that occasions them. Potebnja, to be sure, did not ask such a question, for reasons that can only be speculated about here. The question becames central a few decades later in phenomenological aesthetics, which subjected so-called intentional objects to ontological scrutiny. To Potebnja, the being of such objects, allegedly confirmed by psycholinguistic evidence, was not in question; and yet his definition of the work of poetic art begs such a question. It should be recalled that, while most of his Russian contemporaries defined this work by its effects, he clearly distinguished between its linguistic given and its functional consequences, or, to use phenomenological terminology, between its "intentional structure" and its "aesthetic concretizations." To him, this "structure" was pure and constant form, external and internal, endowed with a variable energy to affect the perceiver's cognition, emotions, and conation. In Russia during the 1860s and 1870s, this was a bold definition even if not carried to its completion. The logical question to ask was, what causes the variability of the work's energy and, thereby, either the dissipation or the increase of its aesthetic relevance? Potebnja did not pose such questions; however, his theory implies that it is the ever-changing historical context, as mediated by our minds, that makes the work of poetic art a clearly contingent or heteronomous phenomenon. It is safe to say, then, that the work of poetic art, as an "intentional structure," is inconceivable without that which it gives rise to. The effects it produces are the foundation of its being. As Ingarden put it, literary art, as an intentional object, "draws

---

[65] Potebnja, *Iz zapisok po teorii slovesnosti*, p. 58.
[66] Ibid.

its existence and its complete bestowal from an intentional experience of consciousness."[67] This prompts the question, do we, and indeed can we, know the work of poetic art without its functional consequences?

Potebnja's theory seems to support both positive and negative answers. On the one hand, it postulates that aesthetic cognition, experience, and awareness depend upon the internal form, and, on the other, that it is cognition that imbues the internal form with aesthetic capacity. This ambiguity unquestionably results from Potebnja's reliance upon psychologism, which prevented him from perceiving intentional objects as heteronomous constructs. Phenomenologists, and particularly Ingarden, have offered a logically sound definition of this problem: The work of poetic art is capable of functioning only in the heteronomous mode of existence.

Independently, the work of poetic art is powerless, without energy. To function, and thereby to be, it must enter into a creative bond with the apperceiving consciousness. On its own, it is not self-sufficient. As pure "intentional structure" it cannot be known. When, however, it is aesthetically perceived, its ontology and teleology become coterminous. And yet its "intentional structure" can be reflected upon, if and when our consciousness knowingly imposes upon itself a series of epistemological limitations, or to use Husserl's language, when it "invalidates all commitments with reference to an experienced object," when it assumes a position of a "disinterested spectator" and "brackets the objective world," and thus seizes the object in question as a "mere phenomenon." Without these limitations, reflective consciousness is incapable of discovering the very essence of the work of poetic art.

Potebnja's theory, as this study has attempted to show, oscillates between psychologistic and phenomenological positions. On the one hand, he stated, very much as the phenomenologists did, that the "general condition of practical observations consists in a possible elimination of everything that impedes it";[68] on the other, however, he held that such impediments, external and internal, and especially the latter, cannot be eradicated entirely. Accordingly, the work of

---

[67] Roman Ingarden, *Spór o isnienie świata,* 2 vols., 2d ed. (Warsaw: Państwowe Wydawnictwo Naukowe, 1960–61), 1:97.

[68] Potebnja, *Iz lekcij po teorii slovesnosti,* p. 464.

poetic art can and cannot be freed entirely from the biases of those who perceive it, and hence can and cannot be known *sui generis*.

In all fairness to Potebnja, we must say that among scholars in the Russian Empire during the second half of the last century, his definition of poetic art was one of the most ideologically neutral. He genuinely strived to define it strictly on its own terms, even though he was not yet prepared to do so radically and at once. Due to this explicit neutrality, Soviet Marxist literary historians have branded Potebnja's "objectivism" as "deeply false."[69] However, any judicial commentary should recognize that for Potebnja, criticism was an intellectual endeavor that does not hastily purge itself of poetry and faith. Its destruction of the poetic and mythical unity of life proceeds *slowly* but *persistently*. In the meantime, criticism "argues with them about their respective boundaries."[70]

---

[69] Cf. G. M. Fridlender, "Osnovnye linii russkoj literaturnoj kritiki ot 90−x godov XIX veka do 1917 goda," in *Istorija russkoj kritiki*, ed. B. P. Gorodeckij et al., vol. 2 (Moscow and Leningrad: AN SSSR, 1958), pp. 415−22.

[70] Potebnja, "Mysl' i jazyk," p. 196.

CHAPTER FIVE

Potebnja's Theory:
Axiomatic System or a
Set of Observational Propositions

Potebnja versus Potebnjanism

Whether Potebnja's theory is an antecedently true axiomatic system, or, instead, a set of propositions that secures its meaning through applicability, would perhaps be an irrelevant issue had Potebnja left a body of critical works. A demonstrated correspondence between his theory and such works would have either proved or repudiated the theory's epistemological cogency. Potebnja, however, produced no such works. His "Preliminary Remarks about L. N. Tolstoj's and F. M. Dostoevskij's Art" does not fill this void, and his numerous references to poetic texts are too disparate to be considered sustained criticism. We are left, as a result, with a series of postulates—untested by their author—concerning the ontology, structure, modality, and function of literary art.

Potebnja's theory is by and large deductive, inasmuch as it proceeds from general propositions to more concrete and specific inferences and systematically cites literary examples to prove their theoretical import. However, while formulating these propositions, Potebnja continuously stressed their epistemological limitations.[1] Such propositions, he observed, were vulnerable to any fact that had not and could not be anticipated, and the quantity of such facts, he also observed, was inexhaustible. To avoid this vulnerability, he held, general propositions "must not become closed configurations," they

---

[1] Potebnja, "Mysl' i jazyk," p. 194.

must remain open-ended. Speaking of psychology as an experimental science, Potebnja wrote:

> If the goal of any science is to explain phenomena that lie within its research competence, then the theory of mental capacities has no scientific character. Concepts of reason, emotions, and will, as generally all concepts formed out of attributes common to many individual phenomena, must say no more than that there are some common attributes in the phenomena examined by us. They should be general and thus indefinite descriptions that replicate what is explicitly depicted by introspection.[2]

If, however, experimental psychology treats these concepts as the actual basis of the phenomena themselves, then it becomes mythology. A number of his propositions, such as, for example, the contention that linguistic and poetic facts are coterminous and can therefore be treated interchangeably, might indeed preclude new facts. Nevertheless we must remember that Potebnja did not present his theory as axiomatically deductive, but rather as a foundation for inferential conclusions. In other words, he did not ascribe to it a final, general value independent of such existential operations as observation and evaluative determination. His general propositions, such as structural affinity between the word and the work of poetic art, the encoded ethnicity in the poetic image, the generative power of the poetic text, the localization of creative and perceptive acts in a psychological rather than in a sociological space, the functional analogy between poetry (verbal arts) and knowledge (scholarship, science)—all seem to be free of deductive pressure. These and other propositions were mediated by inferences drawn primarily from Humboldt and Steinthal's psycholinguistics, and from Herbart and Lotze's intellectualistic psychology. They, in Potebnja's view, could serve as logical conditions in the determination of our knowledge rather than as strictly universal propositions of "if . . . then."

As with most formal systems, it was inevitable that Potebnja's theory would undergo substantive changes at the hands of its adherents. The journal *Voprosy teorii i psixologii tvorčestva,* which initially intended to elaborate and disseminate it, gradually adopted a

---

[2] Ibid., p. 73.

conceptual pluralism. Ostensibly Potebnja's followers were not ready to accept his theory as a set of antecedently valid instruments.

Dimitrij N. Ovsjaniko-Kulikovskij, initially Potebnja's most dedicated follower, came to be his most radical revisionist. What follows here is in no way intended to summarize his extensive scholarship, but rather to highlight the issues on which he parted from Potebnja. In his lectures on the nature of artistic creativity, he defined his method of literary research in this way: "The artist goes from an individual image to the type, and from the type to the idea. This can indeed be called *artistic induction,* and anyone who wants to understand the artist's work must go along the same path of artistic induction. The degree of one's understanding will depend upon the quantity and quality of the data available to him and, of course, upon the extent of his natural creative powers."[3] The exception to this mode of attaining scientific truth is found in symbolist art, "those works of art in which images are not types but *symbols.* The perceiver of such art must, first of all, discover the idea that will in turn provide him with a key to the apprehension of the symbol."[4]

Ovsjaniko-Kulikovskij's position obviously deviates from Potebnja's on a number of points. First, it avows that the creative and critical process begins with a definite image instead of an unknown $X;$ second, it perceives the end of this process as a definite idea, instead of a multi-signifying image; third, it distinguishes image and symbol

---

[3] D. N. Ovsjaniko-Kulikovskij, "Iz lekcij ob osnovax xudožestvennogo tvorčestva," *Voprosy teorii i psixologii tvorčestva* (hereafter *Voprosy;* published irregularly from 1907 to 1923), 1 (Kharkiv 1911, 2d ed.): 14. In and of itself "artistic induction," proposed by Ovsjaniko-Kulikovskij, would not have posed a problem for him had he persisted in it. However, he himself soon discovered its epistemological and methodological limitations. Inasmuch as human characters, minds, and creative powers are different, not to mention the degree in quality and quantity of data necessary for the creation of this or that artistic work, the apprehension of the creative process varies *ad infinitum* from person to person and, in an individual, from age to age. The inevitable conclusion was that knowledge of literary fact, which is deeply embedded in all sorts of collective systems and values, is to be directed toward the predetermined objective. "The subject endeavors to apprehend the work of art first of all *for himself* in the interest of *his* (and not somebody else's) thought, and the entire process is as *intimate* and personal as, for example, are love, anger, conscience, awareness of the accomplished obligation, etc." pp. 11–14. "Iz lekcij ob osnovax xudožestvennogo tvorčestva," ibid., p. 15.

[4] Ovsjaniko-Kulikovskij, "Iz lekcij ob osnovax," p. 14.

as disparate notions. According to Potebnja, the image or symbol, as partial representations of the intended reality, are coterminous. "The poetic image," Potebnja wrote, "may be given the same appellations as those of the image in the word: sign and symbol."[5] In order for it to yield signification, it must be causally contrasted with, or related to, the signified.[6] In the first two processes, the image functions as a simile, metaphor, and synecdoche; in the third, as its means or consequence. All authentic works of poetic art are therefore imaginative or symbolic. Once they lose this quality and are reduced to an external form, they become monosemic, denotative, and prosaic. Ovsjaniko-Kulikovskij, on the other hand, proposed a principally different notion of the poetic image. While for Potebnja it was a structural component of the word, autonomous from consciousness, to Ovsjaniko-Kulikovskij it was an endopsychic experience that reproduces, with some degree of realism, a sensory representation of the intended object. Potebnja insisted on the existential heteronomy of the image, whereas Ovsjaniko-Kulikovskij identified it with the content of the perceiving mind. For Potebnja the semantic transformation of the image into a poetic or prosaic denotation could in time change from a multiple to a single signification, while for Ovsjaniko-Kulikovskij such a transformation was much more determined. By classifying poetic images as typical, symbolic, or schematic, he insisted that "these categories of images can be considered steps leading from poetry to prose."[7] In short, the transition of poetry into prose is orderly and not, as Potebnja contended, fortuitous.

Still another radical departure from Potebnja's theory was Ovsjaniko-Kulikovskij's classification of the creative arts into imaginative (replete with images) and lyrical (without images): "I came to the opposite conclusion about the fundamental difference between lyrical and imaginative arts."[8] The lyrical arts consisted of four basic varieties: verbal, musical, pictorial, and "petrified" (*okamenelyj*)

[5] Potebnja, *Iz zapisok po teorii slovesnosti*, p. 309.

[6] Potebnja, "O nekotoryx simvolax v slavjanskoj narodnoj poèzii," *Èstetika i poètika*, p. 222.

[7] Ovsjaniko-Kulikovskij, *Teorija poèzii i prozy* (Moscow: Izd. I. D. Sytina, 1909), p. 33.

[8] Ovsjaniko-Kulikovskij, "Iz lekcij ob osnovax," p. 1.

which reproduced "imageless thoughts, *emotions,* and *moods.*"[9] The imaginative arts included literary prose and drama, and relied upon images. Art, as a material datum, is merely an external stimulus that excites a variety of cognitive and emotional experiences. Should this be an experience of lyrical emotion (*sentimentum liricum*),[10] the stimulus, inversely, will also be deemed lyrical. Should it be a natural emotion (*sentimentum naturale*), the stimulus will be deemed imaginative. In brief, the criteria for determining the modality of creative arts are strictly psychological. The cognition of the creative arts, as external stimuli, is therefore predicated upon the type of responses they invoke. Accordingly, an a priori definition of these stimuli, no matter how persuasive it might be, is inadequate.

Ovsjaniko-Kulikovskij's understanding of the sources of the creative arts also differed from Potebnja's. While accepting "linguisticity" as the origin of all arts,[11] he at the same time searched for their sources outside of language, particularly in psychophysiology and sociology. Lyrical art, he believed, is rooted in man's psychophysical organization—in the rhythm of the heart, in breathing, in body movements, and in gestures. The diagram on the following page sums up this view.

Unlike Potebnja, Ovsjaniko-Kulikovskij engaged in considerable critical analysis, although his writing reflects little theoretical Potebnjanism. It is, rather, a mixture of psychological, sociological, and ideological conjectures very much in the vein of the Russian criticism of his time. In his *Memoirs,* published posthumously, he wrote: "In 1892/93, I concluded that in scholarship I was to investigate questions of the *psychology of language, of thought, and of creation* and in this connection *the evolution of syntactical forms of language.* It dawned on me that in literature I had to do the *psychological analysis*

---

[9] Ibid., p. 4.

[10] Lyrical emotion, Ovsjaniko-Kulikovskij contended, differs from natural emotion in that it originates in and subsists as an intellectual process. Unlike fear, anger, shame, pity, sorrow, and love, which are rooted in the "sense sphere" and hence are but affective dispositions, *sentimentum liricum* is an experience made up of expressible ideas and systemic sensations. For this reason it "establishes order and harmony in the disorder of thoughts and feelings." "Iz lekcij ob osnovax," p. 10.

[11] Cf. his "Lingvističeskaja teorija proisxoždenija iskusstva i èvoljucija poèzii," *Voprosy* 1 (1911, 2d ed.): 20–33.

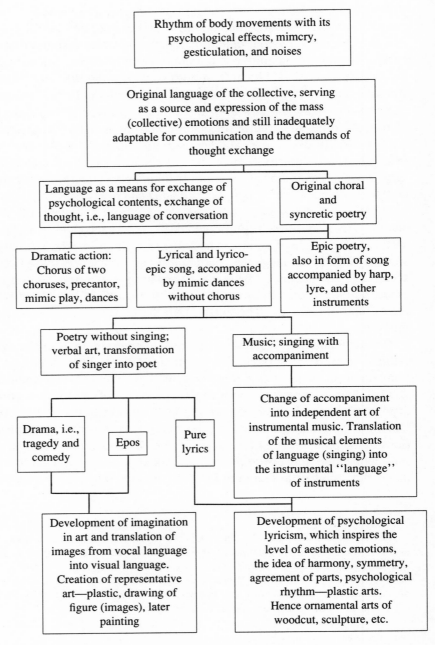

This diagram, Ovsjaniko-Kulikovskij cautioned, should not be ascribed other than methodological significance.

of art and the creativity of great writers and lyrical poets, mainly Russian."[12]

Creative writers, in Ovsjaniko-Kulikovskij's view, fall into one of two categories—observational and experimental. Of the writers he studied, Puškin, Lermontov, Gončarov, Turgenev, Pisemskij, belong to the first category; Gogol', Čexov, and Dostoevskij, to the second. Writers of the first category were capable of containing their predilections and subjective references, and thus reflect reality in its actual givenness. This art, as a result, was an aesthetic analogue of life, history, and human aspirations. Writers of the second category, on the other hand, were preoccupied with their own creativity. For instance, "at the base of all of Gogol's mental work lay an exaggerated hypochondriacal imagination about his shortcomings and even about his largely imagined 'sin.' "[13] The art of these writers is always "from oneself" (*ot sebja*) and "out of oneself" (*iz sebja*), bold in its selection, elimination, and arrangement of sensory data, and licentious in its artistic rendition. Gogol', Ovsjaniko-Kulikovskij observed, projected into his art "his loathsomeness, his search for similar experience in other people, and those of others in himself."[14] His works, consequently, do not present a "broad and comprehensive picture of life, but a *tendentious selection of certain features*."[15] While writing, Gogol' "contemplated and *reacted in torment*, responded in pain, exaggerated and remade those aspects of his soul which he was studying."[16] He looked at the divine world through the prism of his moods, complex and psychologically dark, and to an overstated degree saw nearly everything in man as dark, petty, and narrow."[17] His experimentation with reality, conditioned by "deep mental expression," evidently helped him relieve his inner tensions and thereby achieve emotional catharsis as well as "social importance."[18] Gogol's

---

[12] D. N. Ovsjaniko-Kulikovskij, *Vospominanija* (Petrograd: Vremja, 1923–24), p. 38.

[13] D. N. Ovsjaniko-Kulikovskij, *Sobranie sočinenij,* 9 vols. (St. Petersburg: Izd. I. L. Ovsjaniko-Kulikovskogo, 1912–14), 3: 146.

[14] Ibid., 3: 35.

[15] Ibid., 3: 49.

[16] Ibid., 3: 58.

[17] Ibid., 3: 55.

[18] Ibid.

"abominations,"[19] through creative projection and generalization, were thereby transformed into art.

In contrast, I. S. Turgenev, a representative of the first category, was for Ovsjaniko-Kulikovskij a writer who knew "how to forget himself and turn his eyes to things and persons not only strange but also contrary to what he found in himself."[20] Hence "the analytical aspect in his art is reduced to the minimum, while the descriptive is expressed strongly."[21] It explains little, speculates even less, and depicts vividly. His writing becomes the best possible poetic correspondence of Russian reality. This does not, however, mean that in his art Turgenev circumvented his subjective needs. Unlike Gogol', who subliminally sought purification through creation, Turgenev, Ovsjaniko-Kulikovskij alleged, intentionally sought "those compensatory features (*dopolnenija*) which he himself lacked and which, together with his own assets, would form a harmonious whole."[22] As a man and a writer, he needed Solomin, Bazarov, Rudin, and other imaginary types. Bazarov, Ovsjaniko-Kulikovskij wrote, "represents neither the nihilism of the 1860s nor the replication of the revolutionary type. His personality, *sui generis,* is woven from entirely different elements. . . . By creating him, Turgenev wished to satisfy some urgent and very intimate need of his mind and soul."[23]

The degree of psychological restraint was even greater in Puškin, whose work was—in Ovsjaniko-Kulikovskij's opinion—a model of judiciously controlled poetic art. In this sense, he and Gogol' originated two diametrically opposite trends of nineteenth-century Russian letters: one realistic, attainable by "strict methods, analogous to those in the exact sciences, observation, and experience";[24] and the other impressionistic, attainable through the projection of repressed mental processes or by elevating the *membra disjecta* of the perceived reality into creative focus. Puškin, "in contrast to such *morose geniuses* as Gogol' and Schopenhauer, and like Goethe, was a sociable genius with a very pronounced social disposition . . . he experienced [his

---

[19] Ibid., 3: 35.
[20] Ibid., 2: 35.
[21] Ibid., 2: 287.
[22] Ibid., 2: 35.
[23] Ibid., 2: 58.
[24] Ibid., 6: 141.

emotions] the way actors do when, for example, they portray love on the stage."[25] His poetry dealt with imaginary rather than with his own authentic emotions.

Tolstoj, in Ovsjaniko-Kulikovskij's classification, falls between the two categories. His subjectivity "in his creative process was at one time limited, at another completely removed by objective observation, and then recurred when reality partly justified his hopes and urged him, if only by *hints,* to incarnate in his plebeian characters the process of his own search for truth, of acquiring truth by one's own mind, of freeing the spirit from the limiting and perverting effects of culture—the process he knew well *through* his own inner experience."[26] Tolstoj's vacillation between "Puškinian" and "Gogolian" attitudes, during two ideologically distinct periods of his creative life, assumed different ratios. However, his works, written before 1880— prior to his spiritual crisis—relied primarily upon observation, whereas those written after this period relied upon experiment. Therefore, whereas *War and Peace* was steeped in Tolstoj's observational attitude toward reality, *Anna Karenina* was a product of the experimentation of his mind. Most of what he wrote toward the end of his life was conceived "from the viewpoint of an evangelical religion of love and severe ascetic demands."[27]

Ovsjaniko-Kulikovskij's studies of Čexov, Gercen, Mixajlovskij, Gorkij, Heine, and Goethe follow substantially this same critical line.[28] Their predominantly psychological orientation combines revised Potebnjanism with the psychological views of Th. Ribot, W. Wundt, and L. Lévy-Brühl.

Another follower of Potebnja, Arkadij G. Gornfel'd, upheld Potebnjanism more faithfully than did Ovsjaniko-Kulikovskij. His programmatic article "On the Interpretation of a Work of Art"[29] was an attempt to amplify Potebnja's theory inferentially rather than extraneously. On the question of the language, structure, form, function, creation, and perception of the work of poetic art, Gornfel'd

---

[25] Ibid., 6: 57.
[26] Ibid., 3: 51.
[27] Ibid., 3: 244.
[28] Cf. Ibid., 5: 3 – 221.
[29] A. G. Gornfel'd, "O tolkovanii xudožestvennogo proizvedenija," *Voprosy,* 7 (1916): 1 – 31.

remained close to Potebnja. All genuine works of poetic art, he held, are capacious and potentially polysemous symbols capable of an unrestricted cognitive content, and provide the reader with an apperceptive direction. The inception of such symbols and their transformation into particular signification occurs within the limits of an ethnically constituted consciousness. They arise everywhere, and every time, people speak and think, thereby constituting the very agency of language and thought—the transformation of sensory perception into semantically meaningful propositions. Like communicative or referential scientific signs in a world of infinite diversity, they facilitate the formation of generalizations, systems, and semantic unity. Creative arts, thus, ''are not a luxury, game, or dessert, but a necessity: a precondition of that *cultural synthesis,* of that conciliation of man with society, which ought to crown the new forms of human coexistence.''[30] So long as poetic images or symbols perform such functions, or, to quote Potebnja, ''so long as they function as constant predicates to ever-changing subjects,'' regardless of whether they are ''pure'' or tendentious, they remain artistic. Once they become synonymous with specific references, they become prose. Gornfel'd observed: ''The contents (*idejnoe soderžanie*) of a work of art is the right of the perceiver and not the duty of the creator.''[31] The creation and perception of poetic symbols, Gornfel'd agreed with Potebnja, are identical processes, because their existence is contingent upon their ever-new creation.[32] They ''live'' only ''in the peculiar comprehension of an individual man,'' and their aesthetic value must be validated by a continuous response from readers. As Gornfel'd put it, ''While looking for the genius, we create him. Without his art we suffer; without our creation, (however) he does not exist. . . . The genius resembles God: he is found to the extent that we search for him.''[33]

Gornfel'd wrote about a host of writers—Russian and foreign—including Puškin, Tjutčev, Gogol', Aksakov, V. Ivanov, Belyj, Dostoevskij, Heine, Hugo and Nietzsche. In his criticism he was not always consistent with his own theory. His psychological criticism,

---

[30] A. G. Gornfel'd, ''Buduščee iskusstva'' *Voprosy,* 2 (2d ed. 1910): 181.

[31] A. G. Gornfel'd, *Boevye otkliki na mirnye temy* (Leningrad: Kolos, 1924), p. 9.

[32] Gornfel'd, ''O tolkovanii,'' p. 11.

[33] Gornfel'd, *Boevye otkliki,* pp. 5–17.

unlike psychoanalysis, which persistently discerns between the given and latent intentions of the text, focused only on the former. To Gornfel'd, the poetic text seemed to be semantically one dimensional, free of any consciously or unconsciously concealed significations; consequently, it did not require a special method of elucidation. Texts that contained "indeterminacy of content," such as those of the Russian symbolists, lacked, in Gornfel'd's view, "artistic honesty,"[34] whereas those of Puškin, Tjutčev, Goethe, and Heine, were honest and accessible to direct critical inquiry. When Tjutčev wrote,

> Душе моя—Элизиум теней,
> Теней безмолвных, светлых и прекрасных,
> Ни помыслам годины буйной сей,
> Ни радостям, ни горю не причастных.
>
> My soul—elision of shadows—
> Silent, light, and beautiful shadows,
> Related neither to the intentions of
>   this violent time
> Nor to its joys or sorrows,

he, Gornfel'd claimed, was describing metaphorically the very essence of his soul. Tjutčev's metaphysical poetry "created almost exclusively 'for himself,' to unburden his mind and thereby rationalize his position,"[35] was genuinely confessional. Since his political poetry, on the other hand, did not originate in the "depths of his soul but outside of it,"[36] it was speculative and superficial. In sum, Tjutčev's poetry is resonant with authenticity as well as rhetorical affectation. Criticism need not explain these qualities with additional textual evidence. This poetic dichotomy, for Gornfel'd, reflects Tjutčev's "tragic duality," his two mutually exclusive systems of personality, one questing for solitude and "direct insight into enigmatic issues of existence,"[37] and another searching for the amenities of an efficient bureaucrat and tsarist courtier.

---

[34] Ibid.
[35] A. G. Gornfel'd, *O russkix pisateljax* (St. Petersburg: 1912), p. 4.
[36] Ibid., p. 18.
[37] Ibid., p. 10.

Gornfel'd's study of Puškin's *Mozart and Salieri* attempted to explain what "Mozart and Salieri meant to Puškin and to what moment of his mental life and poetic development this drama came as a response."[38] Without any textual or verifiable evidence, Gornfel'd alleged that Puškin longed to identify himself with Mozart, a true artist, and thereby to exalt himself above the illustrious but shallow poets of his day. The possibility that Puškin's sympathy for Mozart might have been motivated by other reasons was of no interest to Gornfel'd, because to him the concurrence of one's conclusion with the actual state of affairs was neither possible nor necessary. The interpretation of the poetic image, he alleged, very much like the creation of it, was a matter of subjective experience and therefore, as he put it, "the question of which of the two interpretations is correct is not worth posing," Moreover, he stated, "in spite of my conviction that in regard to the work of art different points of view are possible, I will always consider my point of view exclusively correct."[39]

Timofej I. Rajnov, while "inclined to analyze the work of art as a psychological document concerning the artist and his creation,"[40] preferred to act as a "philosopher rather than as a critic or a literary historian."[41] Such a preference, of course, would not have been completely contrary to Potebnja's theory, had Rajnov not stressed philosophy exclusively. Rajnov did this because he believed that Potebnja's goal was to determine the source, the modality, and the collective nature of cognition as well as the exigencies it imposes upon humanity now and for the future.[42] In two studies, one on Gončarov's *Precipice* and the other on Tjutčev's poetry, he elaborated on these issues. Unlike most of Potebnja's followers who had become bogged down in radical psychologism and no longer discerned the created from the creating, Rajnov posited the reality of Gončarov's novel as manifestly different from Gončarov's unconscious projections. Yet while this distinction might have been consistent with

[38] Ibid., p. 151.

[39] Gornfel'd, "O tolkovanii," pp. 27–28.

[40] T. I. Rajnov, "Obryv Gončarova kak xudožestvennoe celoe," *Voprosy*, 7 (1916): 38.

[41] Ibid., p. 32.

[42] T. I. Rajnov, *Aleksandr Afanas'evič Potebnja* (Petrograd: Biografičeskaja biblioteka, 1924), p. 28.

Kant's view on the role of judgment, it did not agree with Potebnja, for whom the demarcation between the creating and the created (or the subjective and objective) was not readily manifest. As Potebnja said, "In a broad as well as strict sense, all properties of [our] mind, although conditioned by the external world, are subjective and remain the result of personal creation."[43] Rajnov, on the other hand, very much in the vein of Kant's theory, held that the faculty of imagination, by continuously resorting to the faculty of judgment, is capable of representing through intuition an object that is itself not present, and thereby can transcend the very act of creation. Poetic creation, in Rajnov's view, is not a blind activity, but, as Kant put it, "a slow and even painful process of improvement, by which [the creator] seeks to render it adequate to his thought, without detriment to the freedom of the play of his powers."[44] The presence of this faculty of judgment in poetic creation enables the poet "to shut himself out" of the very object of his depiction and thus affect the subject/object split. In Rajnov's view, Gončarov's *Precipice* exemplifies such a creative process. Without such demarcation, works of poetic art would be direct extensions of a bound mind.

Boris A. Lezin, the editor of *Voprosy,* interpreted the poetic image as an expression of the mind's attempt to economize its energy, thus linking his view with the "principle of least effort," which was widely accepted in sciences and social sciences toward the end of the nineteenth century.[45] Somewhat earlier, a similar link was already suggested by Ovsjaniko-Kulikovskij. By itself, this link would not have been noteworthy had it not provoked formalists, especially Viktor Šklovskij, to contest it—a contest that subsequently led to the formalist definition of poetic language. As a response to this principle, among others, formalists claimed that poetic language, unlike that of science, is often intentionally retarded or rendered abstruse, and hence attained by the "most effort."[46]

---

[43] Potebnja, "Mysl' i jazyk," p. 195.

[44] Cited in Donald W. Crawford, *Kant's Aesthetic Theory* (Madison: University of Wisconsin Press, 1974), p. 164.

[45] Cf. Boris A. Lezin, "Xudožestvennoe tvorčestvo kak osobyj vid ėkonomii mysli," *Voprosy* 1 (1911, 2d ed.): 202–244.

[46] Cf. V. Šklovskij, "Iskusstvo kak priem," in *O teorii prozy* (Moscow: Federacija, 1929), pp. 7–23.

Another point in Lezin's exposition of Potebnja's theory concerns the role of the unconscious in aesthetic creation and perception. As mentioned above, Potebnja was not sufficiently conclusive about the role of "apperceptive mass" in cognition. Lezin, apparently influenced by psychoanalysis, made the unconscious the *vis major* of the creative process. The sphere of consciousness, according to him, is directly dependent upon the continuous evolvement of the unconscious.[47] Since it is both selective and restrictive of sensory data, in terms of its constituents and functions, the conscious sphere is considerably disproportionate to the unconscious. If only for this disparity, its role in the creative process is ostensibly circumvented. Lezin, however, in contrast to the depth psychologists who attributed poetic creativity almost entirely to repressed factors of the unconscious, saw this sphere more as a dynamic and an ever-expanding reservoir of acquired percepts, which participate in rather than initiate creative activity. In this sense, he remained close to Potebnja.

Perception, reading, and apprehension of art, in Lezin's view, if seen and judged from the perspective of unitary process, can never be interchangeable. This, Lezin added, should not alarm us, since the main significance of art is precisely to affect human diversity rather than to create a sameness. As in speech where the "listener cannot fuse with the speaker [because] one and the same word, conditioned by the diverse reserve of emotions and assumptions, evokes diverse notions (*ujavlennja*),"[48] similarly these acts generate infinite semantic diversity. Hence criticism, too, " is not a matter of an expert who, armed with the experience of his theoretical knowledge, alone is permitted to criticize, while the rest have to listen piously to his words . . . [but rather] it is a matter for all of us, only the degree of the depth of its originality is different."[49]

Lezin's epistemological relativism obviously strays from Potebnja's concept of the word as *tertium comparationis*. Even though Potebnja insisted that all the semantic possibilities of the word or of its analogue, the work of poetic art, cannot be known, an inter-subjectively shared knowledge of the close meaning of the word

---

[47] B. A. Lezin, "Deščo pro teoriju i psyxolohiju slova O. O. Potebni," *Červonyj šljax*, 1925, no. 12, p. 295.

[48] Ibid.

[49] Ibid., p. 296.

certainly can be. "The word," Potebnja wrote, "is as much a means to comprehend the other as it is the means to comprehend oneself. It serves, therefore, as an intermediary among people and establishes among them a reasonable tie, while in an individual it mediates between the new percepts that at a given moment are in consciousness and the previous reserves that are outside of it."[50] By disregarding this contention of Potebnja's, Lezin could claim that the "process of apprehension, of repetition . . . is not equipollent to the process of creation,"[51] and instead maintain that the two processes are inversely correlative.

Toward the end of the 1920s, as Potebnja's theory of literature was assailed more and more by officially sanctioned criticism, Lezin attempted to graft Marxist ideology onto it.[52] Even if the goal behind the attempt was to save Potebnja's theory from suppression, it was doomed to fail, because in 1934, all non-Marxist theories of the creative arts were officially banned in the Soviet Union.

V. I. Xarciev is to be remembered more for the popularization of Potebnja's theory than for any elaboration of it. As an editor of *Iz zapisok po teorii slovesnosti,* his "modest hope was merely to arouse interest in the thoughts of this great scholar."[53]

Other contributors to *Voprosy,* such as A. L. Pogodin, B. M. Èngel'gardt, P. Èngel'meer, and K. Tiander, in spite of their accolades to Potebnja, shared little with his theory. Pogodin's "Language as Art" (Jazyk kak tvorčestvo), for example, implicitly challenged Potebnja's contention about the interdependence of language and thought, and tied his research to the aesthetics of Max Dessoir. Èngel'meer sought the sources of artistic creation in biology and

---

[50] Potebnja, "Mysl' i jazyk," p. 143.

[51] Lezin, "Deščo pro teoriju i psyxolohiju slova," p. 295.

[52] Cf. B. A. Lezin, "O sočetanii psixologičeskogo metoda izučenija xudožestvennogo tvorčestva s marksizmom," *Rodnoj jazyk v škole,* 1927, vol. 6.

[53] V. I. Xarciev, "Èlementarnye formy poèzii," *Voprosy* 1 (1911): 398. Xarciev was also the first to study Potebnja's archives: cf. *Pamjati Aleksandra Afanas'eviča Potebni* (Kharkiv, 1892). Subsequently, in 1922, an examination and description of the archives was done by I. Ja. Ajzenštok, A. V. Vetuxov, B. A. Lezin, K. M. Nemčinova, and O. N. Synjavs'kyj: cf. *Bjuleten' Redakcijnoho komitetu dlja vydannja tvoriv Potebni* (Kharkiv, 1922, no. 1). The third description of Potebnja's archives was published in 1960: cf. Potebnja, A. A. (1835–1891): *Opis' dokumental'nyx materialov ličnogo fonda,* no. 781 (Kiev, 1960).

genetics, and Tiander, in the evolutionary continuum of poetic modalities.

At the outset of this chapter it was suggested that Potebnja's putative definitions were mainly responsible for the emergence of Potebnjanism, a revisionist variant to his theory. Lezin put it this way: "Whereas Potebnja's research in the syntax of the Russian language was systematized, his conclusions about the artistic word had a random character and were not deduced as cautiously as those about syntax. It seemed that their structure was not yet complete; his poetics [therefore] expanded, grew more complex and deep."[54] To this, of course, we should add the ideologically and historically different context of Potebnjanism, as well as the varied intellectual backgrounds and aims of its exponents. The Soviet scholar O. P. Presnjakov wrote: "Representatives of this trend were diverse people with diverse interests and (in terms of their scholarly outlook and talent) with [diverse] views of Potebnja's legacy. Their philosophical and philological positions were quite eclectic and often, unexpectedly, combined the most diverse views on linguistic and literary phenomena. . . . [Hence] none of them could maintain the level of scholarly integrity of thinking, the broadness of views on the evolution of language and literature, that were characteristic of Potebnja."[55] Potebnjanism, to Potebnja's disciples, we conclude, seemed for a short while to provide a schematic coherence, but it soon became a *nomen nudum* for incompatible assumptions about poetic art.

Potebnja and the Symbolists

Russian symbolists of the second generation, who were concerned with the development of symbolist aesthetics—Valerij Brjusov, Vjačeslav Ivanov, Andrej Belyj, and Aleksander Blok—also turned to Potebnja's theory. What made the theory attractive to them was its definition of the word as something on the morphemic level empirically tangible, and, on the semantic, anagogic. These symbolists

[54] Lezin, "Deščo pro teoriju i psyxolohiju slova," p. 291.

[55] O. P. Presnjakov, *A. A. Potebnja i russkoe literaturovedenie konca XIX – načala XX veka* (Saratov: Izd. Saratovskogo universiteta, 1978), p. 142.

therefore concluded that their "mystical cult of symbols"[56] had much in common with such a definition. Andrej Belyj, whose perception of poetic art at various times reflected the philosophical pessimism of Schopenhauer, the existentialism of Nietzsche, the neo-Kantianism of Rickert and Cohen, and the anthroposophy of Steiner, could nevertheless remark that "Potebnja has reached that borderline at which the creed of the symbolist school of poetry begins, and that Russian symbolists would [therefore] put their signature under the words of this outstanding Russian scholar; between him and them there are no contradistinctions, and this shows that Russian symbolists stand on firm ground."[57] Valerij Brjusov regarded Potebnja's theory as the acme of historical development. "Evidently," he observed, "the latest criticism has decisively destroyed all hitherto existing teaching about the final goal of art, including the Aristotelian theory of imitation (mimesis), the Hegelian theory of 'Beauty,' the Schiller-Spencer theory of 'aimless game,' the sensualist theory of personal 'aesthetic gratification,' and the theory of [social] intercourse, defended by Lev Tolstoj. In this way, the field has been cleared so that Potebnja's theory of art, as a special mode of cognition, can establish itself."[58]

To Belyj, Potebnja's definition of the word as an allegedly bifurcated symbol appeared to be the object of exact observation as well as of intuitive apprehension. By confining the word to its external form he meant to sever it from its conventional signification; and by confining it to its internal form, to invoke transcendental reality. This disjunction, however, had inevitably led Belyj to the absolutization of the external and the exaltation of the internal forms. Belyj, for reasons of theoretical expediency, chose to ignore the structural coherence of the word, as conceived by Potebnja, and had thus isolated the two forms from their signification as self-sustaining phenomena. The sounds of the word, he insisted, "are mighty and invariable, beautiful choirs of sounds, occasional sound accords, provoked by reminiscences, woven into the shroud of external illusion; and thus for as long as our cognition does not decompose the sounds completely, the word

[56] J. Holthusen, *Studien zur Ästhetik und Poetik der russischen Symbolismus* (Göttingen: Vandenhoeck und Ruprecht, 1957), p. 22.

[57] Andrej Belyj, *Simvolizm: Kniga statej,* (Moscow: Musaget, 1910), p. 575.

[58] Valerij Brjusov, *Izbrannye sočinenija* (Moscow: Gosudarstvennoe izdatel'stvo xudožestvennoj literatury, 1955), 2: 207.

is not turned into a mute word or mute mathematical sign. We call this illusion cognition."[59] For example, Belyj further observed, "when I call the sound of thunder, which frightens me, *grom,* I create a sound which imitates the thunder (grrr). In creating such a sound it is as if I begin to create the thunder; the process of recreation is cognition; in essence I recognize the thunder."[60] The magic of euphony, he contended, imparts such words with power to penetrate the essences of things; to subordinate them to one's volition; to fight the adverse forces; to resuscitate youth and the primordial, healthy faith in life "from under the debris of a crumbling culture."[61] The thaumaturgic power of the word, Belyj claimed, is also enhanced by its internal form. Depending upon the presence or absence of such forms, there are living words and dead words. The former possess resonant and graphic imagery, the latter, by becoming ideal terms, are but "stinking and decaying corpses."[62] Only the living words are capable of creating dreams and illusions of new realities; living words, used exclusively in poetry, do not prove anything. Through their combination and arrangement, they create objects whose logical meanings are uncertain. As V. Ivanov contended, the image or symbol, as the epicenter of the living word, becomes "infinite in its signification if and when it expresses implications and suggestions by its secret (hierarchical and magical) language: something unverbalizable (*neizglagolaemoe*) and inadequate to the external world. In its ultimate depth it is multifaceted, multicognitive, and always dark."[63] By such language the poet "atavistically perceives and accumulates in himself the reverses of the living antiquity, beautifies all his poetic works . . . and in this way, the symbol becomes an experience of the forgotten and lost property of the national soul."[64]

Needless to say, this perception of the external and the internal forms of the word was at variance with that of Potebnja. Potebnja did not demarcate the two so radically, and he did not ascribe a generative power to the former. "The external form," he stated, "is indivisible

[59] Belyj, *Simvolizm,* p. 438.

[60] Ibid., p. 431.

[61] Ibid., p. 481.

[62] Ibid., p. 436.

[63] V. Ivanov, *Po zvezdam: Stat'i i aforizmy* (St. Petersburg: Ory, 1909), p. 39.

[64] Ibid., p. 40.

from the internal one; it changes along with it and ceases to be itself without it."[65] Articulated sound, he believed, is not determined by a licentious creative act, but by the structural configuration of the word. "In the creation of language," Potebnja wrote, "there is no arbitrariness."[66] The symbolist notion of the poetic image was equally at variance with that of Potebnja, who, while conceiving of it as the principal attribute of poetic language, did not impart to it an exclusive epistemological efficacy. The knowledge generated by poetic language, he wrote, is not antithetic to the knowledge of science. Quite the contrary, "the purpose of poetry is not only to prepare for science, but from time to time to arrange and complete its structure, which has not been raised high [enough] from its ground."[67] In this respect, philosophy and poetry in particular complement one another.

The symbolist view of myths, allegedly also akin to that of Potebnja, was again essentially different. To Potebnja, myth, poetry, and science were mutually evolving and coextensive phenomena. Myth and science, Potebnja wrote, are similar "in that they are acts of conscious thought, acts of cognition to explain X by the aggregate of the previously given attributes, united and brought to consciousness by the word or by the image of A." The first two are equations; the third, correspondence. To the symbolists, on the other hand, myth represented the authentic primordial reality as well as the goal to be achieved through poetic creation.

Valerij Brjusov's definitions of poetry, its linguistic specificity, and its functions did not differ from those of Potebnja as much as Belyj's did. Poetry, he observed, unlike science, which focuses on the empirically verifiable world of matter and experience, is entirely introspective. It begins, he alleged, "at the moment when the artist tries to explain to himself his own secret sensations. Where there is no such explanation, there is no creative art."[68] Consequently, inasmuch as the reality out of which poetry is being spun is the poet himself, its "goal is not communication but self-gratification and self-under-

[65] Potebnja, "Mysl' i jazyk," p. 175.

[66] Ibid., p. 116. Cf. Potebnja's discussion of the symbolism of sounds in "Mysl' i jazyk," pp. 117–22.

[67] Ibid., p. 195.

[68] V. Brjusov, "Ključi tajn," *Vesy* 1 (1904): 3.

standing."[69] In this absolute introspection, however, no matter what symbols the poet chooses to represent himself by, they will always depict a general situation or abstract truth.

In conclusion, two observations can be made: First, the influence of Potebnja's theory upon symbolist aesthetics, except for being its catalyst, is hard to determine; the two theories are manifestly different. Potebnja conceived and formulated his theory as a systematic inquiry into the poetic text, while the symbolists' theory emerged as a mélange of declarative assertions out of a poetic *pursuite de l'inconnaisable,* rather than out of a sustained intellectual quest for knowledge as knowledge. The few rhetorical statements on the merits of Potebnja's theory that the symbolists made are, therefore, not to be taken as evidence of the affinity between the two. Second, genuine agreement between the two theories was hardly possible, because Potebnja professed a unified view of human existence and poetic creation, whereas most of the symbolists held a paradoxical view of the two.

The Formalist Response to Potebnja's Theory

The formalists' initial fascination with and their subsequent disappointment in Potebnja's theory are not the only reasons that Potebnja and the formalists deserve to be brought to a common focus. At issue here is not just the origin of Russian formalism, but also the subsequent origin of structuralism, with its current variants. In 1926, B. M. Éjxenbaum, reviewing "The Theory of the Formal Method," implied the causal relationship between Potebnja and the formalist theory rather explicitly: "At about the time the Formalists emerged, academic scholarship . . . had lost the sense of its own proper object of study to such a degree that its very existence became illusory. . . . The theoretical legacy of Potebnja and Veselovskij, once handed down to their students, was left to stagnate as so much dead capital—a fortune that they were afraid to tap and so caused to depreciate. . . . Against this background, the issues once raised by Potebnja, and accepted on

---

[69] V. Brjusov, "Istiny. (Načala i nameki.)," in *Severnye cvety na 1901 god* (Moscow, 1901), p. 195.

faith by his disciples, revived and took on new meaning."[70]

The issue that was of main concern both to the formalists and to Potebnja was the genus of poetic language. To Potebnja the "poeticalness" of language was synonymous with its demonstrated internal form or mnemonic symbolism. An obliviousness to this form signified "prosaicalness." Such a definition of poetic language, Èjxenbaum observed, once examined against the background of children's language, glossalalia of religious sectarians, "transrational language" (*zaum*) of the futurists, and the like, needed to be redefined. However, in the course of this redefinition, the formalists concluded, Potebnja's view of poetry as "thinking in images" turned out to be "blatantly out of keeping with the facts and in contradiction to the general principles the facts suggested."[71]

What had actually happened was that the formalists, under the impact of futurist experimentation with sound modifications, had shifted their attention from the internal to the external form of poetic language. Viktor Šklovskij explained it this way: "Beyond doubt, the articulatory aspect is a vital component in the enjoyment of a referenceless transrational utterance. It may very well be that a large part of the pleasure poetry gives us stems from its articulatory aspect— from a special dance of the organs of speech."[72] This shift, initially conceived in psychological terms, eventually prompted the formalists to conceptualize the external form in explicitly nonpsychological terms. In brief, as Osip Brik put it, the formalists came to believe that "sounds and sound harmonies are not merely a euphonic extra but are the result of an autonomous poetic endeavor. The orchestration of poetic speech is not fully accounted for by a repertoire of overt euphonic devices, but represents in its entirety the complex product of the interaction of the general laws of euphony. Rhythm, alliteration, and so forth are only the obvious manifestations of particular instances of basic euphonic laws."[73]

---

[70] B. M. Èjxenbaum, "The Theory of the Formal Method," in *Readings in Russian Poetics*, (Cambridge: MIT Press, 1981), pp. 6 – 8.

[71] Ibid., p. 11.

[72] Cited in B. M. Èjxenbaum, "Theory of the Formal Method," p. 10.

[73] Ibid., p. 11.

In order to ascertain the autonomy of the external form, the formalists ascribed to it the capacity to excite the motor receptors of the perceiver and thereby to make him see the external form rather than be cognizant of it. Thus perceptibility (*oščutimost'*) became to them an element of the poetic word. As the phenomenologists would put it, the formalists conceived the poetic object as a phenomenon with its own ontic foundation. The formalist shift to the first component of the poetic language did not result in a complete negation of imagery; it merely meant the reduction of its function to being one of the multiple devices of poetic language. As Šklovskij put it: "One of the means of creating a palpable construction, the very fabric that is experienced, is the poetic image, but it is only one of the means."[74] As such, Šklovskij insisted, it is not so much created as acquired and strategically deployed throughout the poetic text: "Images are handed down, and poetry involves far more reminiscence of images than thinking in them. In any case, imagistic thinking is not that factor whose change constitutes the essence of the momentum of poetry."[75]

Finally, the formalists also challenged Potebnja's position on the function of poetic art. "The aim of art," Šklovskij wrote, "is to give the palpability of the object as a vision and not as a cognition; the devices of art are the devices of 'estrangement' of objects and of impeded form, which increase the difficulty and duration of perception, inasmuch as the process of perception in art is its own end and [hence] must be prolonged; art is a mode of experiencing the making of the thing, whereas [anything] that has already been made is of no importance to art."[76]

The formalists' disenchantment with Potebnja's theory emanated from their ontology of the work of poetic art. Once the formalists detached the external form from its signification and gave it its own semantic efficacy, their deduction of certain theoretical consequences became inevitable. Logically, then, the key concept in Potebnja's theory—the image or internal form—had to be invalidated. But some of their criticism of it was spurred by an obvious misapprehension. For example, Šklovskij criticized Potebnja for not differentiating between poetic and prosaic languages, and consequently between two

---

[74] Ibid., p. 13.
[75] Šklovskij, "Iskusstvo kak priem," p. 8.
[76] Ibid., p. 13.

disparate uses of image—practical and poetic. Ostensibly this criticism had more to do with Ovsjaniko-Kulikovskij's interpretation of Potebnja than with Potebnja himself. As argued above, the validity of Potebnja's theory rested precisely on its explicit discernment of the two languages; however, what distinguished his definition from that of the formalists was its emphasis upon the second component of the poetic word. Nevertheless Potebnja, it may be said, was no less formalist than the formalists themselves. To him, the poeticalness of the poetic text was not determined by anything that has already been made, as Šklovskij said, but rather by its continuous capacity to generate ever-new significations. As a linguistic datum such a text was nothing but form. Its poeticalness, Potebnja claimed, is sustained by its semantic power to be the predicate to an ever-changing subject. The "prosaicalness" of the prosaic language, on the other hand, is indeed determined by something "that has been made." But, to Potebnja both constructs, once perceived, involve cognition, inasmuch as it is impossible to insulate the experience of palpability from cognition. The difference between poetic and prosaic language, if defined in terms of the cognitive effects they have upon the perceiver, is therefore not a matter of palpability versus knowledge but a matter of different *noesis*. In poetic language, internal forms or images are always disproportionate to their signification, while in prosaic language they are either absent or equivalent to their signification.

Such a distinction also invalidates the formalist accusation that Potebnja's theory inadvertently upheld the traditional correlation of form and content. This accusation would have been valid had Potebnja conceived of the two forms—external and internal—and the content they generate as certain paired measures that vary concomitantly, but he certainly did not. The minimal etymological content of the internal form, he claimed, is no more than a stimulus that evokes a variety of contents. Therefore, the two—one manifest and the other potential—cannot be measured. The formalist criticism seems to be more applicable to its own theory: In spite of its claim that in works of creative art only the construction of things rather than things themselves are evident, it nevertheless admits the presence there of "things seen." These works might indeed not have, to use Šklovskij's example, the "stone" as such, but they do have the "stony stone," whereas according to Potebnja they have only the semantic capacity to yield the stone. Translated into more recent linguistic terminology:

According to the formalists, the conversion of signifiers into the signified has already been completed by the poetic text; according to Potebnja, the text awaits completion. Reading, according to the former, is an act accompanied either by astonishment or indifference; according to the latter, reading is an act of discovery.

Although there were other issues in Potebnja's theory to which the formalists reacted critically, it was precisely through reaction that they clearly formulated their own position. Indeed, Èjxenbaum admitted the formalist debt to Potebnja's theory, via *definitio per contra,* by stating that the "clash with the Potebnja doctrine had resulted in a clarification of the basic problems of theoretical poetics."[77]

Potebnja and the Vagaries of Soviet Ideology

In a recent study on Potebnja, the Soviet scholar O. P. Presnjakov observed: "Only a principally new Marxist literary scholarship could genuinely assess the treasure of Potebnja's scientific concepts with their strong and weak aspects; only this scholarship could come close to Potebnja's deep, dialectical understanding of the complex processes of thinking, language, and literature."[78] History, however, does not bear out his claim. Such "new scholarship" has from its official inception been rather distant from Potebnja's aesthetics. In the early 1930s "Potebnja's scientific concepts," together with other non-Marxist theories, were proscribed. In 1938, as eminent a linguist and theorist of literature as V. V. Vinogradov defined Potebnja's aesthetics this way: "The philosophical basis of Potebnjanism is of no use to us; its idealist claims are fragile and rotten."[79] For approximately three decades, virtually no attempt was made to assess his aesthetics critically. In 1968, R. M. Cejlin and A. A. Leontiev, two established Soviet scholars, summed up this sad state of affairs: "During the last few years, with an increased interest in linguistic problems in poetics, one also notices an interest in Potebnja's works in the field. Still missing, however, is an analysis of his poetic concept in light of

---

[77] Èjxenbaum, "Theory of the Formal Method," p. 17.

[78] Presnjakov, *A. A. Potebnja,* p. 178.

[79] V. V. Vinogradov, "A. A. Potebnja," *Russkij jazyk v škole,* 1938, no. 5–6, p. 121.

current aesthetics and theory of literature."[80]

The ideological ban on Potebnja did not extend to his works in linguistics. This same Vinogradov, while condemning the "philosophical basis of Potebnjanism," described Potebnja's linguistic heritage as having "enormous value."[81] In 1941, the Academy of Sciences published the fourth volume of Potebnja's *Notes on Russian Grammar,* and in 1958, reprinted the first two volumes. Shortly after World War II, another noted Soviet linguist, L. A. Bulaxovskij, observed: "Even though more than half a century has passed since his death, he is not just another glorious figure in the history of our linguistics. Potebnja is not the past."[82] What this meant was that Potebnja the linguist was divorced from Potebnja the aesthetician, and as such was readmitted to officially sanctioned scholarship. An implicit challenge to such a separation was made by M. G. Jaroševskij in an article published soon after the war. "Potebnja, who was inclined to philosophical and psychological reflections," Jaroševskij wrote, "cannot be studied only as a linguist. The goal that he posed for the history of language [was] to demonstrate the role of the word in the formation of the consecutive series of systems that comprise the relationship of man toward nature. This aim located the research far beyond the limits of special linguistic problems and thus tied linguistics with philosophy (the theory and history of cognition) and psychology."[83] However, after this correct observation, Jaroševskij did his best to find in Potebnja's theory "spontaneous materialistic elements."[84]

In the 1970s, Potebnja's three principal works on literary theory were republished, albeit in abbreviated form, under the common title *Aesthetics and Poetics.* This renewed attention to his theory of literature did not, however, constitute an official sanction of his ontology and epistemology of the poetic text, because such a sanction would

---

[80] R. M. Cejlin and A. A. Leontiev, "Potebnja, A. A.," *Kratkaja literaturnaja ènciklopedija,* vol. 5 (Moscow: Sovetskaja ènciklopedija, 1968), p. 914.

[81] Vinogradov, "Potebnja," p. 121.

[82] L. A. Bulaxovskij, "Potebnja—lingvist," *Učenye zapiski MGU* 3 (1946), iss. 107, bk. 2: 36.

[83] M. G. Jaroševskij, "Filosofsko-psixologičeskie vozrenija A. A. Potebni," *Izvestija AN, Serija istorii i filosofii* (Moscow), 3, no. 2 (1946): 145.

[84] Ibid., p. 147.

have to entail the restriction of the official demands on this theory. Inasmuch as this was not possible, the only way Potebnja's theory could be included within ideologically safe "legacies" was to dull its neo-Kantianism and stress its alleged materialism. Thus, whereas in the 1930s the "philosophical basis" of the theory had been called "rotten," in the 1970s it was described as a mixture of "materialistic and idealistic tendencies, with the predominance of the latter."[85] Once this definition was made, it became easier to associate Potebnja with the alleged materialism of nineteenth-century Russian radicals.[86] A Soviet Ukrainian aesthetician, M. N. Parxomenko, alleged that in the Ukraine, "Potebnja was the first to approach the issue of the psychology of creativity and the perception of art from the materialistic position. . . . One should, however, remark that materialism and, especially, dialectics in Potebnja's works are not always consistent, that they contain the insurmountable influence of idealistic concepts exerted by contemporary philosophers and psychologists (Steinthal and others). . . . In his works, however, such a way of thinking is a rarity. Its presence does not refute the overall materialistic basis of his linguistic as well as aesthetic views."[87]

Some Soviet scholars, however, have astutely abstained from this attempt to convert Potebnja the neo-Kantian into Potebnja the quasi-materialistic positivist. They have interpreted Potebnja without an explicit ideological bias. The linguist, A. A. Leontiev, for example, observed that Potebnja's linguistics cannot be extirpated from his *Weltanschauung* and then be conceptualized arbitrarily, as an allegedly pure linguistic datum. Because of such extirpations, Leontiev observed, "to date no one has been able to give a convincing

[85] I. V. Ivan'o and A. I. Kolodnaja, "Èstetičeskaja koncepcija A. Potebni," in *Èstetika i poètika*, p. 9.

[86] M. N. Parxomenko, in an introduction to a series of articles on the aesthetic ideas in the Ukraine, stated: "In the course of materialism, the aesthetic views of A. A. Potebnja, an outstanding linguist, literary scholar, and the founder of 'linguistic poetics,' were formed under the considerable influence of Belinskij's, Gercen's, and Černyševskij's ideas." *Istorija èstetiki: Pamjatniki mirovoj èstetičeskoj mysli*, vol. 4, pt. 2 (Moscow: Iskusstvo, 1968), p. 24.

[87] Ibid., pp. 24–26.

analysis of [Potebnja's] linguistic views as part of his overall scientific *Weltanschauung.*"[88]

Many discerning references to Potebnja were made by Vinogradov. In his works on stylistics and poetics, written mostly in the 1950s and 1960s, this prolific Soviet philologist availed himself of Potebnja's various definitions without adjusting them to the prevalent ideological bias. Unlike in the 1930s, when he labeled Potebnja's philosophy of language as being rotten, two and three decades later he observed that, in spite of Potebnja's "subjective-idealist concept of speech" and his "underestimation of the collective basis of the verbal signification in the lexical structure of language,"[89] Potebnja should be recognized for his "remarkable analysis" and his "powerful doctrine." Specifically, Vinogradov accepted Potebnja's view on the similarity of structure in the word and the work of poetic art;[90] he also agreed that "in regard to creative literature, the problem of the image goes back to the explanation of the specificity of verbal images—to images embodied in the verbal fabric of the literary-aesthetic object, which are created from words and by means of words";[91] that the nature of poetic images, regardless of whether they consist of individual words, a paragraph, a chapter, or the entire work, is linguistic. At the same time, Vinogradov disagreed with Potebnja's conclusion concerning the identity of all poetic images. Such an identity, he stated, would render any meaningful taxonomy of literary types virtually impossible. Only their qualitative difference, in Vinogradov's view, permits us to discern the structural and functional specificity of poetic genres. "The structure of the lyrical and the lyricoepic," Vinogradov wrote, "is completely different."[92]

In conclusion, what are the prospects of Potebnja's theory being examined, *sine ira et studio,* by Soviet scholarship? Given the significant changes in Soviet aesthetics during the fifty years of its

---

[88] A. A. Leontiev, *Psixolingvistika* (Leningrad: Nauka, 1967), p. 11.

[89] V. V. Vinogradov, *Iz istorii izučenija russkogo sintaksisa: Ot Lomonosova do Potebni i Fortunatova* (Moscow: Izd. Moskovskogo universiteta, 1958), p. 336.

[90] Vinogradov wrote: "The notion of the internal poetic form extends upon the syntactic structure of the poetic text and upon the construction of the artistic work as a whole." *Stilistika, Teorija poètičeskoj reči, Poètika* (Moscow: AN SSSR, 1963), p. 109.

[91] Vinogradov, *Stilistika, Teorija poètičeskoj reči, Poètika,* p. 336.

[92] Ibid., p. 147.

existence,[93] such a possibility can be neither conclusively projected nor repudiated. As has been shown, in the 1930s Soviet scholarship, due to its quasi-sociological approach, branded Potebnja's theory in scurrilous terms. When, subsequently, that scholarship became more attentive to the aesthetic relevance of the work of poetic art, it at first recognized the historical importance of Potebnja's theory, and then adjusted it to its own current maxims.

Two observations emerge from this treatment of Potebnja's theory. First, Soviet scholarship, even within the limits of its expedient historiography, is no longer relegating it to a "non-event"; at the same time, it cannot assess the theory affirmatively without moderating its ontological and epistemological postulates. Second, in finally recognizing the importance of Potebnja's theory, Soviet scholarship seems as concerned, or even more concerned, with its native (*otečestvennyj*) origin than its general cogency. Thus, we can say that so long as Soviet scholarship conforms to stringent ideological dicta, it will subject Potebnja's theory to a biased interpretation.

---

[93] Cf. Edward M. Swiderski, *The Philosophical Foundation of Soviet Aesthetics: Theories and Controversies of the Post-War Years* (Dortrecht: D. Reidel, 1979).

Conclusion

Many theorists have dreamed of constructing a conceptual model that would subsume and indeed predict an indefinite number of literary works. But insofar as the knowledge of aesthetic objects, unlike that of physical ones, is contingent also upon historically bound values, such a dream has not been realized in full. As I. A. Richards observed somewhat facetiously, above, below, and around theories "can be found other things of value, of service for the appreciation of particular poems and works of art; comment, elucidation, appraisal, much that is fit occupation for the contemplative mind."[1] In any case, a great many conceptual models are but deductive consequences of either varied axiological preferences or of ideologically selected instances. As such they are neither conceptual correspondences nor interpretative tools, but intellectual operations with no mandatory references.

Potebnja was aware of this danger and, as a result, formulated his views in such a way that they could be revised, amended, or even completely invalidated. In his first book, *Mysl' i jazyk,* he already stated that "because the quantity of attributes in every sphere of perception is inexhaustible, the concept cannot become a closed entity."[2] His theory of literature, as a set of concepts, is therefore not nomological, as some of his followers thought it to be. Its status of truth is to be confirmed continuously by concrete works of art. Moreover, as is the case with most literary theories, it contains general propositions whose probability might indeed be zero. For example, one of its propositions is that "art of all time directs [its] efforts toward achieving an

---

[1] I. A. Richards, *Principles of Literary Criticism* (New York: Harcourt, Brace and World, 1928), p. 7.

[2] Potebnja, "Mysl' i jazyk," p. 194.

internal goal,"[3] toward unity of its images. Undoubtedly, there have been and will continue to be poetic texts with contrary intent.

In retrospect, the significance of Potebnja's theory lies not only in how it actually defined the work of poetic art, but also in how it redirected critical attention in the Russian Empire and later in the Soviet Union (and indirectly in Europe) toward issues of the text itself. Generally, then, the principal claims of Potebnja's theory are as follows:

(1) Language and poetic art are genetically related.
(2) Language and poetry have a triune structure.
(3) Internal forms in language and images in poetry have generative power.
(4) Poetry's principal function is cognition.
(5) Aesthetic perception is productive rather than merely reproductive.
(6) Poetry and prose (scholarship and science) are complementary.
(7) Generic taxonomy is arbitrary and serves only heuristic purposes.
(8) Poetic semiosis is predominantly ethnocentric.
(9) Poetic signs and their signification are, as a rule, asymmetrical.
(10) Mythological, poetic, and scientific functions are potentially present in reading, interpretation, and aesthetic experience.

The majority of theoreticians now accept the first claim as valid. Even phenomenological aesthetics, which locates the essence or the invariant constitutive being of the aesthetic object outside the means of its rendition, concedes that the strata of "sound formations" and of "meaning units" in the poetic work of art are grounded in a linguistic context. Hence the affinity between the poetic text and the corresponding linguistic context is a precondition for the emergence of the intersubjectively discernible intentional objects. The language inside poetry, it follows, is coextensive with the language outside of it. Recently even psychoanalytic criticism, which, in the words of Francesco Orlando, used to engage in the "perpetual deciphering of the same few symbols that involve the opposition of phallus and castration, father and mother, the prenatal state and birth, life and death,

---

[3] Potebnja, *Iz zapisok po teorii slovesnosti*, p. 353.

food and excrement,''[4] under the impact of structural linguistics has also shifted its focus to the language of the repressed and thus has admitted the essential contingence of poetic and communicative languages. It was, of course, the formalists, and subsequently the Prague structuralists, who made Potebnja's claim, *mutatis mutandis,* the centerpiece of their aesthetics.

The second and third claims have remained problematical both for formalists and structuralists. In principle, the formalists did not discuss the presence of internal form as the intermediary stratum between the material and the semantic givens of the sign. It exists, they insisted, only occasionally and therefore does not constitute the essential determinant of the poetic sign, nor is it but one of the multiple devices in the inventory of artistic designation. When employed, internal form either retards or enhances the reader's perception, rather than, as Potebnja had it, generating signification. The formalists, however, while downplaying its importance, failed to define its linguistic specificity and thus tended to equate it with tropes. In other words, conceiving the poetic text exclusively from the standpoint of "artistic expediency" (*xudožestvennaja celesoobraznost'*) or artistic function, they underestimated its semantic dimension. In 1960, Roman Jakobson rectified this formalist deficiency by stating that in poetry the internal form is the semantic load of its constituents and as such regains pertinence.[5] In the Soviet Union, Vinogradov, who in the 1920s had shared the formalist position, by the 1950s also agreed that "in regard to creative literature, the problem of the image goes back to the explanation of the specificity of verbal images: the images embodied in the verbal fabric of the literary-aesthetic object that are created from words and by means of words.''[6]

In retrospect, the controversy between Potebnjanists and formalists resulted from the formalists' misunderstanding of Potebnja's concepts of the internal form. They obviously mistook it for a sensory corollary of the word—for a psychological experience that allegedly

---

[4] Francesco Orlando, *Toward a Freudian Theory of Literature, with an Analysis of Racine's* Phedre, trans. Charmaine Lee (Baltimore and London: John Hopkins University Press, 1978), p. 134.

[5] Roman Jakobson, "Closing Statement: Linguistics and Poetics," in *Style in Language,* ed. Thomas A. Sebeok. (Cambridge: MIT Press, 1960), p. 376.

[6] Vinogradov, *Stilistika, Teorija poètičeskoj reči,* p. 94.

generates signification. And insofar as they were eager to free their inquiry into poetic language from psychologism, Potebnja's concept had to be invalidated. However, as this study has shown, Potebnja's theory of the internal form had nothing to do with sensory corollaries. Internal forms in language and images in poetic texts are linguistic constants and hence not subject to psychological unpredictability. Unlike the external forms that endure in time, they get "used up" and disappear. But so long as they persevere, they are observable sign-vehicles with a semantic load.

The fourth claim, in terms of what we know now about the functions of language and poetic texts, seems to be somewhat dated. To Potebnja, meaning, in addition to articulated sound, was an indispensable condition of the word and, by analogy, of the poetic text. Meaning was not synonymous with reference, however. On the contrary, explicit reference, he insisted, limited its "poeticalness" and enhanced its "prosaicalness." Poetry, to him, was explicitly equated with polysemy, and prose with assertion. But even this qualification hardly makes it applicable to texts that on either the planes of expression or intended content are equivocal or semantically restrictive—which elicit a distinct experience of a *je ne sais quoi*. Potebnja's claim therefore is relevant only for texts that retain semiotic potentiality. To put it differently, poetic texts must not transcend that semantic limit beyond which they cease to function cognitively.

The fifth claim is fairly consonant with recent theories of perception, and particularly with that of Roman Ingarden, presented in his seminal work, *The Cognition of the Literary Work of Art*. Aesthetic reaction to the text does indeed involve a whole range of adjustments and interpretative processes and, in this sense, is productive rather than simply reproductive. Potebnja's claim, however, is not to be thought of as antithetical to the realist view of the direct confrontation with the presented object. This object, Potebnja insisted, is given in the text, but, as a rule, only attributively, through a partial representation. Its configurative occurrence in consciousness is not *ex nihilo,* but out of the tangible givens provided by the text. Aesthetic perception is, therefore, a creative transformation of the minimally given poetic imagery. These images, both as linguistically given and as aesthetically transformed, are as a result asymmetrical, a fact that provides for their ever-new qualitative and quantitative variations and even for their dissolution.

The sixth claim, if understood strictly within Potebnja's definition of prose and science—as polysemous and monosemous texts—appears to be too general to have an all-inclusive epistemological importance. If, however, we conceive of poetry and science as but two major modalities of man's cognitive involvement with himself and his world, as Potebnja did, then his view of their relations should not be dismissed lightly. In the context of modern science, which no longer distinguishes between matter and energy, Potebnja's insistence on the functional correlation of the two through the concept of *energeia* may in fact impress us as quite *au courant*.

The seventh claim is merely a logical extension of the sixth. It stipulates that, insofar as the genus of the poetic text is determined by the function of its internal form, classification based on its appearance is arbitrary. Accordingly, there are but two major textual classes: poetry and prose. Inevitably, such classification extends the notions of "poeticalness" upon all polysemous and "prosaicalness" upon all explicitly referential texts. Potebnja must have become aware of the inadequacy of such a taxonomy, because he also proposed classification based on the external form. Hence lyrical poetry, as cognition that objectivizes feelings, is characterized by brevity, consciousness, verbal incompletion, and lyrical disorder; drama, by a non-narrative, dialogical language; and epic, by a language without leaps and gaps.

The eighth claim may also be of limited applicability now, for its strictly genetic approach to the semantic derivations hardly works with supranational texts. This claim, by equating individual mind with the specific collective consciousness, implies one and the same source of polysemy. The encoding and decoding of poetic texts, accordingly, are determined and limited by the same source, the same vision of reality. In view of this, Potebnja could say that apprehension of the poetic work is but an inverted creation, or that its material and semantic structures originate in the same mnemonic experiences. If, however, we revise this claim—as, for example, Baxtin did—by perceiving the internal form of the text as being anchored in the historical, ideological, and aesthetic orders whose linguistic designations are not identical with those of ethnic order, then it may gain broader applicability.[7] But even in its original formulation, this claim argues

---

[7] Mixail Baxtin, reacting to what he called the "hegemony of language over the

against the semantic void of the text. Unlike de Saussure, who claimed that neither the materialization of thoughts nor the spiritualization of sounds existed, Potebnja infers that poetic creation and poetic perception are not totally fortuitous processes, but are aroused, directed, and indeed limited by the internal forms of their language.

The ninth claim, given the etymological character of semiological signs, is both logical and necessary. The artistic signifier is always less than its signified, because the latter results not merely out of the grammatically ordered signs, but also out of the diachronically constituted words or out of the intersubjectively or collectively shared meanings. Structuralists since de Saussure have contested this view, because they conceived of communicative signs as having only a dual character. However, when de Saussure stated that "language is always a legacy," and, more recently, Roland Barthes that "in language the link between signifier and signified is contractual in its principle, but this contract is collectively inscribed in a long temporality,"[8] then structuralists seemed to reintroduce into their consideration the once abhorred diachrony.

---

perception and conceptualization of reality" wrote: "But even in those eras where the absolutism of this hegemony has long since been displaced—in the already historical epoch of language consciousness—a mythological feeling for the authority of language and a faith in the unmediated transformation into a seamless unity of the entire sense, the entire expressiveness inherent in that authority, are still powerful enough in all higher ideological genres to exclude the possibility of any *artistic* use of linguistic speech diversity in the major literary forms. The resistance of a unitary, canonic language, of a national myth bolstered by a yet unshaken unity, is still too strong for heteroglossia to relativize and decenter literary and language consciousness. This verbal-ideological decentering will occur only when a national culture loses its sealed-off and self-sufficient character, when it becomes conscious of itself as only one among *other* cultures and languages. It is this knowledge that will sap the roots of a mythological feeling for language, based as it is on an absolute fusion of ideological meaning with language; there will arise an acute feeling for language boundaries (social, national and semantic), and only then will language reveal its essential *human* character. . . . Language, no longer conceived as a sacrosanct and solitary embodiment of meaning and truth, becomes merely one of many possible ways to hypothesize meaning." M. M. Bakhtin, "Discourse in the Novel," in *The Dialogic Imagination,* ed. Michael Holquist (Austin: University of Texas Press, 1981).

[8] Roland Barthes, *Elements of Semiology* (Boston: Beacon Press, 1967), p. 51.

The last claim, although offered primarily as a counterargument to Max Müller's position on myth as a disease of language, is strikingly analogous to Ernst Cassirer's treatment of expression. To both Potebnja and Cassirer, image in myth asserts its primacy over the thing, and thus expresses rather than signifies it. "In myth," Cassirer wrote, "the given does not consist primarily in the merely sensuous, in a complex of sensory data, which are only animated and made meaningfully a subsequent act of mythical apperception. The expressive meaning attaches to the perception itself in which it is apprehended and immediately experienced."[9] Potebnja said exactly the same thing when he observed that myth consists in the transposition of individual attributes of the image that is expected to explain the phenomenon (or a series of phenomena) into a phenomenon itself. In other words, in myth, the phenomenon and image, no matter how detached they might be perceptually, are coterminous. There is, however, one thing that distinguishes Potebnja's position from that of Cassirer. To Potebnja "language was the principle protoplastic means of mythical thinking."[10] Without language, myth simply does not and cannot exist. To Cassirer, on the other hand, both myth and language are impediments to the "pure ether of thought" or "witnesses of human inadequacies," and as such must be transcended. "Philosophical knowledge," he wrote, "must first free itself from the constraint of language and myth."[11] Such transcendence, however, in Potebnja's view, is hardly possible, for thought and language are concurrent processes. "In vain," he wrote, "some people try to fence off science from mythic thought by sharp and immovable boundaries because the difference between them lies only in degree."[12] Also, "myth is related to scientific thinking in that it, too, is an act of the conscious thought, an act of cognition to explain X by the aggregate of the previously given attributes, united and brought to consciousness by the word or by the image of A."[13] And yet myth, poetry, and science, even if only for heuristic reasons, are in Potebnja's view to be demarcated as three distinct modalities of creative quest. They might

---

[9] Cassirer, *Philosophy of Symbolic Forms,* 3: 68.
[10] Potebnja, *Iz zapisok po teorii slovesnosti,* p. 433.
[11] Cassirer, *Philosophy of Symbolic Forms,* 3: 16.
[12] Potebnja, *Iz zapisok po teorii slovesnosti,* p. 280.
[13] Ibid., p. 418.

dispute, Potebnja wrote, their respective boundaries, but they must also maintain a certain equilibrium among themselves, because its violation causes suffering to man.[14]

* * * * *

Potebnja's theory remains persistently viable. Proposed over a century ago, in an environment hardly conducive to its survival and growth, the theory has withstood the tribulations of time and has retained its exegetical efficacy. Seven of its ten claims or inferences seem to be ostensibly consonant with the currently prevalent views of myth, language, poetic art, and referential prose.

Today, regardless of whether we share the position on literary theory of Northrop Frye or I. A. Richards—whether we insist on literary theory's absolute indispensability or on its temporal limitations—we recognize the cogency of the former and the arbitrariness of the latter, and we ascribe to the former the power of general proposition. A great many of Potebnja's definitions are cogent, and as such merit our attention.

[14] Potebnja, "Mysl' i jazyk," p. 196.

Bibliography

I. Works of Potebnja

Potebnja, A. A.

Autobiographical note. In Pypin, A. N., *Istorija russkoj ètnografii,* vol. 3. St. Petersburg: M. M. Stasjulevič, 1891.

———— "Černovye zametki o L. N. Tolstom i F. M. Dostoevskom." *Voprosy teorii i psixologii tvorčestva,* 1914, vol. 5.

———— *Iz lekcij po teorii slovesnosti: Basnja, poslovica, pogovorka.* Kharkiv: K. Sčasin, 1894. Slavic Printings and Reprints, 150. The Hague: Mouton, 1970.

———— *Iz zapisok po russkoj grammatike.* Vols. 1, 2. Moscow: Gos. učebno-ped. izd., 1958. Vol. 3. Moscow: Prosveščenie, 1968. Vol. 4. Moscow and Leningrad: AN SSSR, 1941.

———— *Iz zapisok po teorii slovesnosti: Poèzija i proza. Tropy i figury. Myšlenie poètičeskoe i mifičeskoe. Priloženija.* Kharkiv: Izd. M. F. Potebni, 1905. Slavic Printings and Reprints, 128. The Hague: Mouton, 1970.

———— "Jazyk i narodnost'." In *Iz zapisok po teorii slovesnosti.* Kharkiv: M. Zil'berg, 1905.

———— *Malorusskaja narodnaja pesnja po spisku XVI veka: Tekst i primečanija.* Voronež: V. I. Isaev, 1877.

———— "Mysl' i jazyk." In *Èstetika i poètika,* compiled by I. V. Ivan'o and A. I. Kolodnaja. Moscow: Iskusstvo, 1976. *Mysl' i jazyk* was originally published in 1862, and republished in 1892, 1913, 1922, 1926.

_____ *Narodnye pesni Galickoj i Ugorskoj Rusi, sobrannye Ja. F. Golovackim.* St. Petersburg: Imp. akademija nauk, 1880.

_____ *O dole i srodnyx s neju suščestvax.* Moscow: 1867.

_____ *O kupal'skix ognjax i srodnyx obrjadov i poverij.* Moscow: 1865.

_____ *O mifičeskom značenii nekotoryx obrjadov i poverij.* Moscow: 1865.

_____ *O nekotoryx simvolax v slavjanskoj narodnoj poèzii.* 2d ed. Kharkiv: 1914.

_____ *O svjazi nekotoryx predstavlenij v jazyke.* Voronež: V. I. Isaev, 1867.

_____ *Ob'' jasnenija malorusskix i srodnyx narodnyx pesen': Koljadki i ščedrovki.* Warsaw: M. Zemkevic, 1887.

_____ "Osnovy poètiki." *Voprosy teorii i psixologii tvorčestva,* 1910, vol. 2.

_____ "Otryvki iz perevodov 'Odissei'." In *Iz zapisok po teorii slovesnosti.* Kharkiv: M. Zil'berg, 1905.

_____ *Pereprava čerez vodu, kak predstavlenie braka.* Moscow: 1868.

_____ "Psixologija poètičeskogo i prozaičeskogo myšlenija." *Voprosy teorii i psixologii tvorčestva,* 1910, vol. 2.

_____ *Slovo o polku Igoreve: Tekst i primečanija A. Potebni.* Voronež: V. I. Isaev, 1878.

_____ *Udarenie.* Ed. by V. Ju. Frančuk. Kiev: Naukova dumka, 1973.

II. *European Sources of Potebnja's Theory*

Benfey, Th.

       Pantschatantra: Fünf Bücher indischer Fabeln, Märchen und Erzählungen. Leipzig: F. A. Brockhaus, 1873.

Carriere, M.

    Die Poesie: Ihr Wesen und ihr Formen mit Grundzügen der vergleichenden Literaturgeschichte. Leipzig: F. A. Brockhaus, 1864.

Curtius, G.

    Grundzüge der griechischen Etymologie. Leipzig: B. G. Teubner, 1873.

Drobisch, M. W.

    "Über Lotze's psychologischen Standpunkt." In *Zeitschrift für Philosophie von Fichte und Ulrici,* vol. 2, no. 34.

Fischer, Kuno.

    Geschichte der neueren Philosophie. Mannheim: Basserman und Mathy, 1854.

Grimm, J. L.

    Deutsche Mythologie. Vols. 1 – 3. Berlin: Harwitz und Gossman, 1875 – 1878.

    ———— *Über den Ursprung der Sprache.* Berlin: Akademie der Wissenschaften, 1851.

Gubernatis, A. de

    Die Tiere in der indogermanischen Mythologie. Leipzig: F. W. Grunow, 1874.

Herbart, J. F.

    Lehrbuch zur Einleitung in die Philosophie. Königsberg: A. Unzer, 1834.

Herder, J. F.

    Abhandlung über den Ursprung der Sprache. Berlin: S. F. Voss, 1772.

Heyse, K. W. L.

    System der Sprachwissenschaft. Berlin: F. Dümmler, 1856.

Humboldt, W.

    Gesammelte Schriften. 17 vols. Berlin: Königliche Preussische Akademie der Wissenschaften, 1903 – 1936.

Kuhn, A.

    Über Entwicklungsstufen der Mythenbildung. Berlin: Akademie der Wissenschaften, 1873.

Lazarus, M.

Das Leben der Seele in Monographien über seine Erscheinungen und Gesetze. Berlin: F. Dümmler, 1856.

Lessing, G. E.

Abhandlungen über die Fabel. Vienna: Franz Prosch, 1867.

Lotze, H.

Mikrokosmus, Ideen zur Naturgeschichte und Geschichte der Menschheit: Versuch einer Anthropologie. 3 vols. Leipzig: Hirzel, 1856 – 1864.

Mommsen, Ty.

Die Kunst des deutschen Übersetzers aus neueren Sprachen. Leipzig: A. Gumprecht, 1858.

Paul, H.

Prinzipien der Sprachgeschichte. Halle: A. S., M. Niemeyer, 1880.

Rudiger, L.

"Über Nationalität." *Zeitschrift für Völkerpsychologie und Sprachwissenschaft,* 1865, vol. 3.

Schleicher, A.

Die Sprachen Europas in systematischer Übersicht. Bonn: H. B. König, 1850.

Steinthal, H.

"Assimilation und Attraktion." *Zeitschrift für Völkerpsychologie und Sprachwissenschaft,* 1860, vol. 1.
_____ *Einleitung in die Psychologie und Sprachwissenschaft.* Berlin: F. Dümmler, 1871.
_____ "Das Epos." *Zeitschrift für Völkerpsychologie und Sprachwissenschaft,* 1868, vol. 5.
_____ *Grammatik, Logik und Psychologie: Ihre Prinzipien und ihr Verhältnis zu einander.* Berlin: F. Dümmler, 1850.
_____ "Die Sage von Prometheus." *Zeitschrift für Völkerpsychologie und Sprachwissenschaft,* 1862, vol. 2.

———— "Über den Wandel der Leute und des Begriffs." *Zeitschrift für Völkerpsychologie und Sprachwissenschaft,* 1880, vol. 1.

———— *Der Ursprung der Sprache in Zusammenhang mit den letzten Fragen allen Wissens.* Berlin: F. Dümmler, 1858.

———— "Zur Sprachphilosophie." *Zeitschrift für Völkerpsychologie und Sprachwissenschaft,* 1875, vol. 8.

Taine, H. A.

Philosophie de l'art. Paris: G. Baillière, 1872.

Tajlor, E.

Pervobytnaja kul'tura: Issledovanija razvitija mifologii, filosofii, religii, iskusstva i obyčaev. St. Petersburg: 1873.

Vogüé, E. M.

Le roman russe. Paris: B. Plon, Nourrit et cie, 1886.

Wackernagel, W.

Poetik, Rhetorik und Stilistik: Akademische Vorlesungen. Halle: Ludwig Sieber, 1873.

Waitz, Th.

Lehrbuch der Psychologie als Naturwissenschaft. Braunschweig: P. Vieweg, 1849.

Zeitschrift für Völkerpsychologie und Sprachwissenschaft. Edited by G. von M. Lazarus and H. Steinthal. 1860–1889, 20 vols. Berlin: F. Dümmler.

III. *Works by Potebnjanists*

Gornfel'd, A. G.

"A. A. Potebnja i sovremennaja nauka." *Letopis' Doma literatorov,* 1921, no. 4.

———— "A. A. Potebnja. Iz lekcij po teorii slovesnosti. Basnja. Poslovica. Pogovorka." *Severnyj vestnik,* 1894, no. 12.

———— "A. A. Potebnja, k 30-letiju so dnja ego smerti." In *Boevye otkliki na mirnye temy.* Leningrad: Kolos, 1924.

———— "Buduščee iskusstva." *Voprosy teorii i psixologii tvorčestva*, 1910, 2d ed., vol. 2.

———— "Iz stat'i muki slova." *Voprosy teorii i psixologii tvorčestva*, 1911, 2d. ed., vol. 1.

———— "Lekcii A. A. Potebni. Iz vospominanij byvšego slušatelja." *Pamjati A. A. Potebni: Sbornik Xar'kovskogo istoriko-filologičeskogo obščestva*, vol. 4. Kharkiv: 1892.

———— *Novye slovečki na starye slova.* Petrograd: Kolos, 1922.

———— *O russkix pisateljax.* St. Petersburg: 1912.

———— "O tolkovanii xudožestvennogo proizvedenija." *Voprosy teorii i psixologii tvorčestva*, 1916, vol. 7.

———— *Puti tvorčestva.* Petrograd: 1922.

Lezin, B. A.

———— "Deščo pro teoriju i psyxolohiju slova O. O. Potebni." *Červonyj šljax*, 1925, no. 1 – 2.

———— "O sočetanii psixologičeskogo metoda izučenija xudožestvennogo tvorčestva s marksizmom." *Rodnoj jazyk v škole*, 1927, vol. 6.

———— "Opisanie rukopisej A. A. Potebni." In *Bjuleten' Redakcijnoho komitetu dlja vydannja tvoriv Potebni* (Kharkiv), 1922, no. 1.

———— "Xudožestvennoe tvorčestvo kak osobyj vid èkonomii mysli." *Voprosy teorii i psixologii tvorčestva*, 1911, 2d ed. vol. 1.

Ovsjaniko-Kulikovskij, D. N.

———— "A. A. Potebnja kak jazykoved-myslitel'." *Kievskaja starina*, 1893, vol. 42, pt. 7, pp. 3 – 46; pt. 8, pp. 269 – 89; pt. 9, pp.342 – 60.

———— "Filosofija jazyka v trudax A. A. Potebni." *Sbornik Xar'kovskogo istoriko-filologičeskogo obščestva*, 1893, vol. 5.

———— "Iz lekcij ob osnovax xudožestvennogo tvorčestva." *Voprosy teorii i psixologii tvorčestva*, 1911, 2d ed., vol. 1.

———— *Jazyk i iskusstvo.* Kharkiv: 1895.

_____ "Lingvističeskaja teorija proisxoždenija i èvoljucija poèzii." *Voprosy teorii i psixologii tvorčestva*, 1911, 2d ed., vol. 1.

_____ "Lirika kak osobyj vid tvorčestva." *Voprosy teorii i psixologii tvorčestva*, 1910, 2d ed., vol. 2.

_____ "Nabljudatel'nyj i èksperimental'nyj metod v iskusstve." *Vestnik Evropy*, 1903, no. 4.

_____ *Sobranie sočinenij.* Moscow: Gosudarstvennoe izd., 1923 – 24.

_____ *Teorija poèzii i prozy: Teorija slovesnosti.* Moscow and Petrograd: Gosudarstvennoe izdatel'stvo, 1923.

_____ *Voprosy psixologii tvorčestva.* St. Petersburg: D. E. Žukovskij, 1902.

_____ *Vospominanija.* Petrograd: Vremja, 1923.

Pogodin, A. A.

_____ "Jazyk kak tvorčestvo." *Voprosy teorii i psixologii tvorčestva*, 1913, vol. 4.

Rajnov, T. I.

_____ *Aleksandr Afanas'evič Potebnja.* Petrograd: Kolos, 1924.

_____ "Obryv Gončarova kak xudožestvennoe celoe." *Voprosy teorii i psixologii tvorčestva*, 1916, vol. 7.

Vetuxiv, O.

_____ "Toward an Understanding of Potebnja." *Annals of the Ukrainian Academy of Arts and Sciences in the U.S.*, 1956, vol. 5, no. 2 – 3, pp. 1029 – 1111.

Vetuxov, A.

_____ "Do rozuminnja Potebni." *Naukovyj zbirnyk Xarkivs'koji naukovo-doslidnoji katedry istoriji Ukrajiny*, 1926, no. 2 – 3.

_____ "Etnolohično-etnohrafični roboty Potebni." *Zapysky Xarkivs'koho instytutu narodnoji osvity*, 1928, vol. 3.

_____ *Iz vospominanij ob A. A. Potebne odnogo iz poslednix ego slušatelej R. I. Kaširennova.* Kharkiv: 1913.

_____ *Jazyk, poèzija i nauka.* Kharkiv: 1894.

_____ "Potebnjanstvo." *Rodnoj jazyk v škole*, 1923, bk. 1, pp. 110 – 16: bk. 2, pp. 106 – 108.

_____ "Sumcov ta potebnjanstvo." *Naukovyj zbirnyk Xarkivs'koji naukovo-doslidnoji katedry istoriji Ukrajiny*, 1924, no. 1.

_____ "Z arxivu Potebnjans'koho komitetu: Uryvky, lystuvannja z Potebneju, ščo stosujut'sja ukrajins'koho pravopysu." *Zapysky istoryčno-filolohičnoho viddilu VUAN*, 1927, bk. 13–14.

Voprosy teorii i psixologii tvorčestva.
Edited by Boris Lezin. Kharkiv, 1907–1923, 8 vols.

Xarciev, V. I.

"Èlementarnye formy poèzii." *Voprosy teorii i psixologii tvorčestva*, 1911 (2d ed.), vol. 1.

_____ "Mifotvorčestvo, poèzija i nauka." *Voprosy teorii i psixologii tvorčestva*, 1914, vol. 5.

_____ "Mova ta pys'menstvo—javlinnja odnoho gatunku." *Červonyj šljax*, 1925, no. 8.

_____ "Novyj trud po istorii jazyka i mysli A. A. Potebni." *Trudy Pedagogičeskogo otdela pri Xar'kovskom istoriko-filologičeskom obščestve*, 1899, no. 5.

_____ "Potebnja i sučasna poetyka." *Červonyj šljax*, 1927, no. 12.

_____ "Predislovie." In Potebnja, A. A., *Iz zapisok po russkoj grammatike.* Vol. 3. Kharkiv: 1899.

_____ "Predislovie." In Potebnja, A. A., *Iz zapisok po teorii slovesnosti.* Kharkiv: 1905.

_____ "Učenie A. A. Potebni o narodnosti i nacionalizme." *Mirnyj trud,* 1902, vol. 2, pp. 179–69; vol. 3, pp. 170–181; vol.5, pp. 118–38.

_____ "Vstupna stattja odnoho iz učniv Potebni." In Potebnja, A. A., *Polnoe sobranie sočinenij,* vol. 1: *Mysl' i jazyk.* Odessa: 1926.

IV. *Works on Potebnja and his Theory*

Ajzenštok, I. Ja.

"Bezsonovščyna: Z materijaliv do žyttjepysu O. O. Potebni." *Zapysky istoryčno-filolohičnoho viddilu VUAN,* 1928, bk. 16.

_____ "Ešče o Jagiče i Potebni." *Bjuleten' Redakcijnoho komitetu dlja vydannja tvoriv Potebni* (Kharkiv), 1922, no. 1.

_____ "Potebnja i Manžura." *Zapysky istoryčno-filolohičnoho viddilu VUAN*, 1929, bk. 21/22.

_____ "Potebnja i my." *Žyttja i revoljucija*, 1926, no. 12.

_____ "Potebnja i ukrajins'ka literatura." *Šljaxy mystectva*, 1921, no. 2.

_____ and Synjavs'kyj, A. N. "Opisanie rukopisej A. A. Potebni." *Bjuleten' Redakcijnoho komitetu dlja vydannja tvoriv Potebni* (Kharkiv), 1922, no. 1.

Bahalij, D.

"Dumky O. O. Potebni pro ukrajins'ku narodnist'." *Bjuleten' Redakcijnoho komitetu dlja vydannja tvoriv Potebni* (Kharkiv), 1922, no. 1.

_____ "Oleksandr Opanasovyč Potebnja: Zahal'na xarakterystyka." *Červonyj šljax*, 1924, no. 4–5.

_____ "Pohljady O. Potebni na rol' nacmovy v utvorenni kul'tury." *Zapysky Xarkivs'koho instytutu narodnoji osvity*, 1928, vol. 3.

Beletskij, A.

"Potebnja i nauka istorii literatury v Rossii." *Bjuleten' Redakcijnoho komitetu dlja vydannja tvoriv Potebni* (Kharkiv), 1922, no. 1.

Belyj, A.

"Mysl' i jazyk: Filosofija jazyka A. A. Potebni." *Logos*, 1910, bk. 2.

_____ *Simvolizm: Kniga statej*. Moscow: Musaget, 1910.

Berezin, F. M.

"K voprosu o filosofskix osnovax lingvističeskoj teorii A. A. Potebni." In *Metodologičeskie problemy istorii jazykoznanija*. Moscow: 1974.

Bilodid, O. I.

"Filosofs'ki osnovy lingvistyčnoji koncepciji O. O. Potebni." *Movoznavstvo*, 1975, no. 5, pp. 9–19: no. 6, pp. 12–21.

_____ "Včennja O. Potebni pro značennja slova." *Movoznavstvo*, 1967, no. 4.

150   *Potebnja's Psycholinguistic Theory of Literature*

———— "Vklad O. O. Potebni u vitčyznjanu movoznavču nauku: Do 60–x rokovyn z dnja smerty." *Naukovi zapysky Kyjivs'koho deržavnoho universytetu,* 1951, vol. 10, no. 3.

Bobkova, V. S.
"O. O. Potebnja—doslidnyk narodnoji poetyčnoji tvorčosty." In *Oleksandr Opanasovyč Potebnja: Juvilejnyj zbirnyk do 125 riččja z dnja narodžennja.* Kiev: 1962.

———— "O. O. Potebnja pro xudožnju symvoliku narodnoji poeziji." *Narodna tvorčist' ta etnohrafija,* 1960, no. 4.

Budagov, P. A.
Slovo i ego značenie. Leningrad: 1974.

Bulaxovskij, L. A.
Aleksandr Afanas'evič Potebnja: K 60–lettiju so dnja smerti. Kiev: 1952.

———— "Lingvističeskoe nasledstvo A. A. Potebni." *Russkij jazyk v škole,* 1952, no. 2.

———— "Lingvistyčna spadščyna O. O. Potebni." *Visti AN URSR,* 1942, no. 1–2.

———— "Movoznavec'-myslytel'." *Ukrajins'ka literatura,* 1941, no. 1–2.

———— "Potebnja–lingvist." *Učenye zapiski MGU,* 1956, vol. 3, no. 107.

Buzuk, P. A.
Očerki po psixologii jazyka. Odessa: 1918.

Cejlin, R. M.; Leontiev. A. A.
"Potebnja, A. A." In *Kratkaja literaturnaja ènciklopedija,* vol. 5. Moscow: Sovetskaja ènciklopedija, 1968.

Čexovyč, K.
Oleksander Potebnja: ukrajins'kyj myslytel'-lingvist. Warsaw: Ukrajins'kyj naukovyj instytut, 1931.

Čudakov, A. P.
"A. A. Potebnja." In *Akademičeskie školy v russkom literaturovedenii.* Moscow: 1975.

Čyčerin, O. V.

"Včennja O. O. Potebni pro literaturnyj styl'." In *O. O. Potebnja i dejaki pytannja sučasnoji slavistyky: Materialy*. Kharkiv: 1962.

Drozdovskaja, E.

"Potebnja, A. A." In *Literaturnaja ènciklopedija,* vol. 9. Moscow: Izd. Kommunističeskoj akademii, 1935.

Efimec, V. D.

"Problema edinstva xudožestvennogo i naučnogo myšlenija v èstetike xar'kovskoj psixologičeskoj školy." *Vestnik MGU, Filosofija,* 1974, no. 1.

Èjxenbaum, B.

"Teorija formal'noho metodu." *Červonyj šljax,* 1926, no. 6–7.

Erlich, V.

Russian Formalism: History–Doctrine. The Hague: Mouton, 1955.

Filin, F. P.

"Metodologija lingvističeskix issledovanij A. A. Potebni." In *Jazyk i myšlenie.* Moscow and Leningrad: 1935.

_____ "Predislovie." In Potebnja, A. A., *Iz zapisok po russkoj grammatike,* vol. 4. Moscow and Leningrad: AN SSSR, 1941.

_____ "Potebnja i sučasne movoznavstvo." *Movoznavstvo,* 1975, no. 5.

Finkel', O.

"Peredmova." In Potebnja, O., *Z lekcij po teoriji slovesnosty: Bajka, prysliv'ja, prypovidka.* Kharkiv: 1920.

Fizer, J.

"Conceptual Affinities and Differences between A. A. Potebnja's Theory of Internal Form and Roman Ingarden's Stratum of Aspects." In *Contributions to the VIIth Int. Congress of Slavists, Linguistics and Poetics, Vol. 1. Warsaw, 1973.* The Hague: Mouton, 1973.

_____ *Psychologism and Psychoaesthetics: A Historical and Critical View of Their Relations.* Amsterdam: John Benjamin B. V., 1981.

Frančuk, V. Ju.

"Bibliohrafija prac'." *Oleksandr Opanasovyč Potebnja.* Kiev: Naukova dumka, 1975.

_____ "Do pytannja vyvčennja rukopysnoji spadščyny O. O. Potebni." In *O. O. Potebnja i dejaki pytannja sučasnoji slavistyky: Tezy dopovidej i povidomlen' III Respublikans'koji slav''jans'koji konferenciji.* Kharkiv: 1960.

_____ *Oleksandr Opanasovyč Potebnja.* Kiev: Naukova dumka, 1975.

Glants, M. M.

"O ponjatii vnutrennej formy slova v trudax A. A. Potebni." *Voprosy filosofii i sociologii* (Leningrad), 1971, no. 3.

Hutjakulova, V. A.

"Nekotorye problemy obraznogo myšlenija A. A. Potebni." In *Aktual'nye problemy èstetiki i xudožestvennogo proektirovanija.* Moscow: 1970.

_____ "Xudožestvennoe proizvedenie i slovo v traktovke A. A. Potebni." *Voprosy teorii i istorii èstetiki* (Moscow), 1970, no. 6.

Ivan'o, I.

"Pytannja zmistu i formy v doslidžennjax z estetyky u 20-x rokax." In *Z istoriji filosofs'koji dumky na Ukrajini.* Kiev: 1965.

Ivan'o, I. and Kolodnaja, A.

"Èstetičeskaja koncepcija A. Potebni." In Potebnja, A. A., *Èstetika i poètika.* Moscow: Iskusstvo, 1976.

Jagič, I. V.

"Istorija slavjanskoj filologii." In *Ènciklopedija slavjanskoj filologii,* no. 1. St. Petersburg, 1910.

Jaroševskij, M. G.

"Filosofsko-psixologičeskie vozrenija A. A. Potebni." *Izvestija AN SSSR, Serija istorii i filosofii,* 1946, vol. 3, no. 2.

———— "Ponjatie vnutrennej formy slova v Potebni." *Izvestija AN SSSR,* 1946, vol. 5, no. 5.

Kacnel'son, S. D.

"K voprosu o stadijal'nosti v učenii Potebni." *Izvestija AN SSSR,* 1948, vol. 7, no. 1.

Kogan, S. Ja.

"Filosofskie voprosy lingvističeskoj koncepcii Potebni." In *Oleksandr O. Potebnja, 1835–1960: Tezy dopovidej i povidomlen'.* Odessa: 1960.

Kolodna, A. I.

"Dejaki pytannja metodolohiji istoriji filosofiji i osoblyvosti doslidžennja filosofs'kyx osnov naukovoji spadščyny O. O. Potebni." In *Z istoriji filosofiji na Ukrajini.* Kiev: 1967.

———— "Èlementy dialektiki v lingvističeskoj koncepcii A. A. Potebni." In *Tezy dopovidej XXI naukovoji sesiji Černivec'koho universytetu, Sekcija filolohičnyx nauk.* Černivci: 1965.

———— "Filosofskaja koncepcija A. A. Potebni." *Tezisy dokladov XXI naučnoj sessii Černovitskogo universiteta, Sekcija obščestvennyx nauk.* Černivci: 1963.

Krymskij, S. B.

"Potebnja, A. A." *Filosofskaja ènciklopedija.* Moscow: Sovetskaja ènciklopedija, 1967.

Kublanov, B.

Gnozeologičeskaja priroda literatury i iskusstva. Lviv: L'vivs'kyj deržavnyj universytet, 1958.

Lachman, R.

"Potebnja's Concept of Image." In *The Structure of the Literary Process.* Ed. P. Steiner, M. Červenka, and R. Vroon. Amsterdam and Philadelphia: John Benjamin, 1982.

Lafarriere, D.

"Potebnja, Šklovskij, and the Familiarity/Strangeness Paradox." *Russian Literature,* 1976, vol. 4.

Ljapunov, B. M.

"Vospominanija o A. A. Potebne." *Živaja starina,* 1892, no. 1.

Maškin, A. P.

"Kritičeskie vozrenija Potebni." *Bjuleten' Redakcij-noho komitetu dlja vydannja tvoriv Potebni* (Kharkiv), 1922, no. 1.

⸻ "Na šljaxu do naukovoji estetyky." *Šljaxy mystectva*, 1922, no. 1.

⸻ "Potebnja." *Šljaxy mystectva*, 1921, no. 2.

Medvedev, F. P.

"O. O. Potebnja ta joho naukova dijal'nist'." *O. O. Potebnja i dejaki pytannja sučasnoji slavistyky: Tezy dopovidej i povidomlen' III Respublikans'koji slav''jans'koji konferenciji.* Kharkiv: 1960.

Melkumjan, P. L.

"Izobrazitel'nye sredstva russkogo jazyka v issledo-vanijax A. A. Potebni." *Naučnye trudy Erevanskogo universiteta, Serija filologičeskix nauk*, 1954, vol. 42, no. 3.

Naukova spadščyna O. O. Potebni i sučasna filolohija. Edited by V. Ju. Frančuk. Kiev: Naukova dumka, 1985.

Ostrjanyn, D. X.

"Filosofs'ke značennja naukovoji spadščyny O. O. Potebni." In *Oleksandr Opanasovyč Potebnja, Juvilejnyj zbirnyk do 125 – riččja z dnja narodžennja.* Kiev: 1962.

Pelex, P. M.

"Pytannja vzajemozvjazku myslennja i movy v pracjax O. O. Potebni." In *Narysy z istoriji vitčyznjanoji psyxolohiji kincja XIX i počatku XX st.* Kiev: 1959.

Petrov, V.

"Do pytannja pro Potebnju i Lotze." *Zapysky istoryčno-filolohičnoho viddilu VUAN*, 1926, bk. 9.

⸻ "O. Potebnja—folkl'oryst." *Ukrajins'kyj zasiv*, 1943, no. 4.

⸻ "Potebnja i Lotze." *Zapysky istoryčno-filolohičnoho viddilu VUAN*, 1924, bk. 4.

Plotnikov, I. P.

"Obščestvo izučenija poètičeskogo jazyka i Poteb-nja." *Pedagogičeskaja mysl'*, 1923, no. 1.

Popov, P. M.
    "Do xarakterystyky naukovoji dijal'nosti Potebni."
    Radjans'ke literaturoznavstvo, 1947, no. 7–8.

Presnjakov, O. P.
    A. A. Potebnja i russkoe literaturovedenie konča XIX–načala XX veka, Saratov: Izd. Saratovskogo universiteta, 1978.

————— "O. O. Potebnja i problema zvyčnoho slovovžyvannja v xudožn'omu movlenni." *Movoznavstvo,* 1975, no. 5.

————— *Slovo, dumka, obraz: Pro filolohičnu spadščynu.* Kiev: 1974.

Pustovojt, P. G.
    "Učenie A. A. Potebni i sovremennye teorii obraza." In *Ot slova k obrazu.* Kiev: 1974.

Rjadčenko, N. G.
    "A. A. Potebnja o vnutrennej forme slova." In *Oleksandr Opanasovyč Potebnja, 1835–1960: Tezy dopovidej i povidomlen'.* Odessa: 1960.

Rozenberg, O. H.
    "Do xarakterystyky filosofičnyx pohljadiv O. O. Potebni." *Naukovyj zbirnyk Xarkivs'koji naukovo-doslidnoji katedry istoriji Ukrajiny,* 1926, no. 2–3.

————— "Z poetyky O. O. Potebni." *Potebnja i dejaki pytannja sučasnoji slavistyky: Tezy dopovidej i povidomlen' III Respublikans'koji slav''jans'koji konferenciji.* Kharkiv: 1960.

Šamraj, A. O.
    "Potebnja i metodolohija istoriji literatury." *Naukovyj zbirnyk Xarkivs'koji naukovo-doslidnoji katedry istoriji Ukrajiny,* 1924, no. 1.

Shevelov, G. Y.
    "Alexander Potebnja as a Linguist." *Annals of the Ukrainian Academy of Arts and Sciences in the United States,* 1956, vol. 5, no. 2–3.

Škljarevs'kyj, H. I.
    "Pohljady O. O. Potebni na estetyčno smišne: Vyvčennja movnyx zasobiv komičnoho." In *O. O. Potebnja i dejaki pytannja sučasnoji slavistyky: Materialy.* Kharkiv: 1962.

Šklovskij, V.

"Iskusstvo kak priem." In *O teorii prozy*. Moscow: Federacija, 1929.

_____ "Potebnja." In *Poètika: Sborniki po teorii poètičeskogo jazyka*. vol. 1. Petrograd: 1919.

Smirnov, A. A.

"Puti i zadači nauki o literature." *Literaturnaja mysl'*, 1923, no. 2.

Sosina, R. V.

"A. A. Potebnja o značenii slova." *Učenye zapiski Rjazanskogo ped-instituta*, 1962, vol. 30.

Sumcov, N. F.

"A. A. Potebnja." In *Ènciklopedičeskij slovar' Brokhauza-Èfrona*, vol. 24. St. Petersburg: 1898.

_____ "Do istoriji naukovoho vplyvu O. Potebni." *Naukovyj zbirnyk Xarkivs'koji naukovo-doslidnoji katedry istoriji Ukrajiny*, 1926, no. 2–3.

_____ "Spisok pečatnyx sočinenij A. A. Potebni i otzyv o nix." *Pamjati A. A. Potebni: Sbornik Xar'kovskogo istoriko-filologičeskogo obščestva*, vol. 4. Kharkiv: 1892.

Tenjanko, Ju. P.

"Potebnja pro piznaval'nu funkciju mystectva." *Filosofs'ka dumka*, 1975, no. 1.

Vinogradov, V. V.

"A. A. Potebnja." *Russkij jazyk v škole*, 1938, no. 5–6.

_____ "Grammatičeskaja koncepcija A. A. Potebni." In *Sovremennyj russkij jazyk*. Moscow: 1938.

_____ "K sporam o slove i obraze." *Voprosy literatury*, 1960, no. 5.

_____ *Stilistika, Teorija poètičeskoj reči, Poètika*. Moscow: AN SSSR, 1963.

_____ "Učenie A. A. Potebni o stadijal'nosti razvitija sintaksičeskogo stroja v slavjanskix jazykax." *Vestnik MGU*, 1946, no. 3–4.

_____ *Voprosy marksistskoj poètiki*. Leningrad: 1936.

Vol'ter, E. A.

"Potebnja. Bibliografičeskie materialy dlja biografii Aleksandra Afanas'eviča Potebni." In *Sbornik otdelenija russkogo jazyka i slovesnosti—Instituta Akademii nauk.* Vol. 53, no. 8. St. Petersburg: 1892.

Vygotskij, L. S.

Psixologija iskusstva. Moscow: Iskusstvo, 1968.

Wellek, René.

A History of Modern Criticism. Vol. 4. New Haven and London: Yale University Press 1965.

Weststeijn, W. G.

"A. A. Potebnia and Russian Symbolism." *Russian Literature,* 1979, vol. 7.

Žirmunskij, V.

Voprosy teorii literatury: Stat'i, 1916–26. Leningrad: Academia, 1928.

V. *Other Works Cited in this Study*

Bakhtin, M.

The Dialogic Imagination. Edited by Michael Holquist. Austin: University of Texas Press, 1981.

Barthes, R.

Elements of Semiology. Boston: Beacon Press, 1967.

Brjusov, V.

Izbrannye sočinenija v dvux tomax. Moscow: Gosudarstvennoe izdatel'stvo xudožestvennoj literatury, 1955.

Cassirer, E.

The Philosophy of Symbolic Forms. 3 vols. New Haven and London: Yale University Press, 1973.

Crawford, D. W.

Kant's Aesthetic Theory. Madison: University of Wisconsin Press, 1974.

Croce, B.

Aesthetic as Science of Expression and General Linguistic. New York: Noonday Press, 1962.

Fichte, J. G.
    Reden auf die deutsche Nation. Berlin: Deutsche
    Bibliothek, 1912.
Fridlender, G. M.
    "Osnovnye linii russkoj literaturnoj kritiki ot 90-x
    godov XIX veka do 1917 goda." In *Istorija russkoj
    kritiki.* Vol. 2. Moscow and Leningrad: AN SSSR,
    1958.
Goethe, Johann W.
    Sämtliche Werke, 40 vols. Stuttgart and Berlin: T. G.
    Cotta, 1902–1907.
Herder, J. G.
    Sämtliche Werke. 33 vols. Berlin: Bernhard Suphan,
    1877–1913.
_____ *Sprachphilosophische Schriften.* Hamburg: F. Mei-
    ner, 1960.
Holthusen, J.
    *Studien zur Ästhetik und Poetik der russischen Sym-
    bolismus.* Göttingen: Vandenhoech und Ruprecht,
    1957.
Ingarden, R.
    Spór o isnienie świata. Warsaw: Państwowe Wydaw-
    nictwo Naukowe, 1960.
Ivanov, V.
    "Po zvezdam." *Opyty filosofskie, èstetičeskie i kri-
    tičeskie.* St. Petersburg: Ory, 1910.
Jakobson, R.
    "Closing Statement: Linguistics and Poetics." In
    Style in Language edited by T. Sebeok. Cambridge:
    MIT Press, 1960.
Jauss, H. R.
    Positionen der Negativität. Edited by H. Weinrich.
    Munich: Wilhelm Fink Verlag, 1975.
Leontiev, A. A.
    Psixolingvistika. Leningrad: Nauka, 1967.
Lessing, G. E.
    *Laokoon oder über die Grenzen der Malerei und
    Poesie.* Berlin: C. F. Voss, 1766.

Mukařovský, Jan.
> *The Word and Verbal Art: Selected Essays.* Translated by John Burbank and Peter Steiner. New Haven and London: Yale University Press, 1977.

Orlando, F.
> *Toward a Freudian Theory of Literature with an Analysis of Racine's Phedre.* Baltimore and London: John Hopkins University Press, 1978.

Peirce, C. S.
> *The Collected Papers of Charles Sanders Peirce,* 8 vols. Cambridge: Harvard University Press, 1931–58.

Richards, I. A.
> *Principles of Literary Criticism.* New York: Harcourt, Brace and World, 1926.

Špet, G.
> *Vnutrennjaja forma slova: Ètjudy i variacii na temy Gumbol'dta.* Moscow: Gosudarstvennaja akademija xudožestvennyx nauk, 1923.

Swiderski, E. M.
> *The Philosophical Foundation of Soviet Aesthetics: Theories and Controversies of the Post-War Years.* Dortrecht: D. Reidl, 1979.

Tiemann, Barbara.
> *Fabel und Emblem.* Munich: Wilhelm Fink Verlag, 1974.

Tynjanov, Ju.
> "Rhythm as the Constructive Factor of Verse." In *Readings in Russian Poetics: Formalist and Structuralist Views,* edited by Ladislav Matejka and Krystyna Pomorska. Cambridge: MIT Press, 1971.

Weisgerber, L.
> "Die inhaltbezogene Grammatik." In *Von den Kräften der deutschen Sprache,* vol. 3. Düsseldorf: Pädagogischer Verlag Swann, 1953.
> _____ "Die sprachliche Erschliessung der Welt." In *Von den Kräften der deutschen Sprache,* vol. 3. Düsseldorf: Pädagogischer Verlag Swann, 1953.

Whorf, B.

"The Relation of Habitual Thought and Behavior to Language." In *Language, Culture and Personality: Essays in Memory of Edward Sapir,* edited by L. Spier et al. Menasha, Wisc.: Sapir Memorial Publ. Fund, 1941.

Index

Aesop, 68
Afanas'ev, Aleksandr N., 58n
Ajzenštok, I. J., 119n
Aksakov, Ivan S., 114
Auerbach, Erich, 2

Barthes, Roland, 138
Batteux, Charles, 72
Baxtin, Mixail, 21, 137
    137n – 138n
Belyj, Andrej, 94, 114, 120,
    121 – 122
Blok, Aleksandr, 120
Braithwaite, R. B., 81n
Brik, Osip, 125
Brjusov, Valerij, 120, 121,
    123 – 124
Bühler, Karl, 80n
Bulaxovskij, L. A., 129
Buslaev, F. I., 20 – 21

Cassirer, Ernst, 4, 8 – 9, 32n, 139
Cejlin, R. M., 128
Černyševskij, Nikolaj G., 102
Čexov, Anton, 111, 113
Cognition
    criticism and, 97 – 101
    poetry and, 82 – 91
    of self, 86 – 87, 89
Cohen, Hermann, 121

Content. *See* under
    Poetry; Speech
Corrozet, Gilles, 65n
Criticism, as form of cognition,
    97 – 101
Croce, Benedetto, 2, 3, 25
    on aesthetics, 2 – 3

Derrida, Jacques, 56
Dessoir, Max, 119
Dobroljubov, Nikolaj A., 102
Dostoevskij, Fedor, 101, 111,
    114
Dramatic Poetry, 62 – 63
Drobisch, Moritz, 82

Eco, Umberto, 78
Èjxenbaum, B. M., 124, 125,
    128
Èngel'gardt, B. M., 119
Èngel'meer, P., 119 – 120
Epic, 61 – 62
Erlich, Victor, 1
Etymology, 31, 52
Expression, poetry and, 91 – 94

Fable, 63 – 70
    Lessing's view of, 63 – 66, 68
    and proverb compared,
        70 – 71

Fet, A. A., 41
Fichte, J. G., 32n
Folklore, 54–55
Form
    external, 38–40
    immanent, 51–60
    intentional, 60–63
    internal, 40–44
    See also Poetry; Speech
Formalists, 75–76, 80n,
    124–128
Fridlender, G. M., 104n
Frye, Northrop, 140

Genre. *See* Form, intentional
Gercen, Aleksandr I., 113
Goethe, J. W. von, 112, 113, 115
    on drama, 61n
Gogol', N., 85, 111, 112, 114
Gončarov, Ivan A., 111, 116
    Precipice, 116–117
Gorkij, Maxim, 113
Gornfel'd, Arkadij G., 113–116

Hegel, G. W. F., 121
Heine, Heinrich, 42n, 113, 114,
    115
Herbart, Johann, 82, 106
Herder, Johann G., 32n, 71–72,
    73, 74
Hofstadler, A., 81n
Holquist, Michael, 21n
Holthusen, J., 121n
Hugo, Victor, 114
Humboldt, Wilhelm, 1, 2, 4, 8,
    10, 16–17, 18–19, 20–21,
    24, 26, 29–30, 92, 106
    on translation, 37
Husserl, Edmund, 27

Imagery. *See* Poetry, internal
    form of
Ingarden, Roman, 11, 102, 103n,
    137
Ivan'o, I. V., 20n
Ivanov, Vjačeslav, 114, 122, 129

Jakobson, Roman, 135
James, William, 86
Jaroševskij, M. G., 129
Jauss, Hans R., 94

Kant, Immanuel
    aesthetic theory of, 60
    epistemology of, 3, 4
Kantemir, A. D., 72
Kantian philosophy, 74
    representation in, 8
    and role of judgment, 117
Kašerinov, V. I., 7
Kolodnaja, A. I., 20n
Krylov, I. A., 68, 72
Krymskij, S., 5

La Fontaine, Jean de, 68
Language, as symbolic correlate
    to reality, 9
Lazarus, Moritz, 1
Leontiev, A. A., 128, 130–131
Lermontov, Mixail, 42n, 87n,
    93, 100, 111
Lessing, Gotthold, 13–14,
    63–64
    analysis of fables, 63–66, 68
Lévy-Brühl, L., 113
Lezin, B. A., 7, 117–119, 120
Lotze, Hermann, 1, 81, 82, 106
Lyric, 62

Metaphor, 56–57
Metonymy, 57
Mixajlovskij, N. K., 113
Mukařovský, Jan, 46, 75–76, 80n, 95
Müller, Max, 58n, 139
Myth, 58
  distinguished from poetry, 59–60

Nagel, E., 81n
Nemčinova, K. M., 119n
Nietzsche, Friedrich, 114, 121

Orlando, Francesco, 134
Ostrjanyn, D. X., 2
Ovsjaniko-Kulikovskij, D. N., 107–113, 117, 127
  on the arts, 108–110
  on creativity, 111
  criticism by, 109, 111
  on poetic image, 108

Parxomenko, M. N., 130
Peirce, Charles S., 3
Perry, R. B., 81n
Phaedrus, 66, 68n
Pisarev, Dimitrij I., 102
Pisemskij, Aleksej F., 111
Poetry
  as activity, 11–14
  auxiliary functions of, 94–97
  and cognition, 82–91
  constituents of, 36–37
  content of, 44–47
  distinguished from myth, 59–60
  and expression, 91–94
  external form of, 38–40
  as form, 16–19
  genres of, 61–63
  imagery, teleology of, 79–82
  internal form of, 40–44
  language and, 29–36
  as narration, 14–16
Pogodin, A. L., 119
Potebnja, Alexander
  East Slavic language studies of, 6–7
  life
    birth of, 6
    death of, 7
    education of, 6
  philosophy
    algorithm of poetry, 79–80, 88–94
    analysis of fable and proverb, 63–75
    formalist view and, 75–76, 80n, 124–128
    function of language, 9–10
    Marxian assessment of, 2, 104, 128–132
    ontology of, 23–26
    relation between language and poetry, 29–38
    symbolist view and, 120–124
    20th century revisionist views of, 106–120
    views on poetry, 11–23
    word as analogue to poem, 19–23
  works
    Lectures on the Theory of Literature, 7
    Notes on Russian Grammar, 7

Notes on the Theory of Literature, 7
On the Mythological Significance of Some Rituals and Super-stitions, 6
Preliminary Remarks about Tolstoj's and Dostoevskij's Art, 78, 100, 106
Thought and Language, 6, 29, 133
Presnjakov, O. P., 2, 120, 128
Proverb, 70 – 71
Puškin, Aleksandr, 100, 111, 112, 114, 115
Mozart and Salieri, 116

Rajnov, Timofej I., 116 – 117
Ribot, T., 113
Richards, I. A., 133, 140
Rickert, Heinrich, 121

Sapir, Edward, 5
de Saussure, Ferdinand, 4, 30, 139
Schiller, J. C. F. von, 61n, 121
Schopenhauer, Arthur, 112, 121
Semantic decoding, 3
Signification, 34 – 36
Šklovskij, V., 22n, 75, 80n, 94, 117, 125 – 127
Speech, form and content of, 30 – 34
Spencer, Herbert, 121
Špet, Gustav, 40n
Spitzer, Leo, 2, 3
Steiner, Rudolf, 121

Steinthal, Heymann, 1, 4, 8, 33n, 43n, 106
Structuralism, 4
Sumarokov, A. P., 72
Swiderski, Edward M., 132n
Symbolism. *See* Poetry, internal form of
Symbolists, 120 – 124
Synjavs'kyj, O. N., 119n

Tiander, K., 119, 120
Tiemann, Barbara, 65n
Tjutčev, Fedor, 42n, 87n, 114, 115, 116
Tolstoj, L. N., 99n, 100, 113, 121
Translation, 37
Tredjakovskij, V. K., 72
Turgenev, Ivan, 65, 111, 112
Tynjanov, Jurij, 19 – 20

Veselovskij, Aleksandr N., 58n
Vetuxov, A. V., 7, 119n
Vinogradov, V. V., 128 – 129, 131, 135
Vogüé, E. M., 100 – 101
Vossler, Karl, 2

Waitz, Theodor, 82
Weisgerber, Leo, 5, 32n
Wellek, René, 1
Whorf, Benjamin, 5
Wundt, W., 113

Xarciev, V. I., 7, 119